The Lens Of The Father

Gaining Clarity by Restoring the Optics of My Heart

Dennis G. Lindsay

Copyright © 2024 by Dennis G. Lindsay

All rights reserved

The Lens Of The Father - *Gaining Clarity by Restoring the Optics of My Heart*

No part of this publication may be reproduced, stored in a retrieval system or transmitted in any form or by any means, electronic, mechanical, photocopying, recording, scanning or otherwise, except as permitted under code 107 or 108 of the 1976 United States Copyright Act, without the prior written permission of the authors.

ISBN: 978-1-949565-95-9

Adam DiLernia
Book Cover Designer & Graphic Consultant
Seedsprout Consulting, LLC

Printed in the United States of America

Dedication

I dedicate this book in loving memory of my grandmother, Maggie, who not only led me to Christ, but dedicated her life to worshipping Jesus wholeheartedly. Her commitment to prayer, forgiveness and faithful service to others had a tremendous impact on my life, ministry and worldview. This paved the way for me to become the man of God that I am today and global leader in the Body of Christ.

Table of Contents

Chapter 1 - My "HIS" Story.................................1

Chapter 2 - Hidden Nuggets............................11

Chapter 3 - Truth vs. Fact.................................19

Chapter 4 - Through a Child's Eyes.................25

Chapter 5 - The Orphan Heart........................35

Chapter 6 - Identity is Everything..................43

Chapter 7 - Breakthrough................................51

Chapter 8 - Sonship..59

Chapter 9 - Redeeming Love..........................69

Chapter 10 - I can see clearly now.................79

Chapter 11 - All things work together..........87

Chapter 12 - The Challenge............................93

Acknowledgments

To Wynne Goss, I'm extremely grateful that you are my spiritual father. Your guidance and unwavering support, especially throughout the process of writing this book, have been priceless. I deeply honor the wisdom you have shared over the years and cherish our covenant relationship. I also extend my sincerest thanks to my spiritual mother, Gwenda Goss, for your steadfast prayers and support. Thank you both very much. Your influence has been pivotal in bringing this book to completion.

To my beautiful wife of 31 years, Kathleen, words cannot fully express my gratitude for your unwavering support throughout this journey. It was your prayers and faithful support that would enable me to complete this work as God has called me to do.

To my dear brother in Christ, Steven England, I want to express my heartfelt gratitude for the key role you played in the development of this book. Our partnership in ministry, both here and abroad, has been invaluable.

To my wonderful children—Dennis Jr., Amber, Terrel (son-in-love), and Christopher and also my five grandchildren—I am tremendously honored and blessed to be your father and "pop pop". I love each of you dearly and I am very excited to see you all walk in generational blessings.

To my faithful friends and mentors, Carl and Sheila Riley, I am deeply thankful for our covenant connection that has spanned for over thirty years. Your godly wisdom and support will always be cherished.

To all my spiritual children who have served faithfully in ministry, thank you for your prophetic words, love and support throughout the years. May God's generational blessings continue to overflow in your lives.

Foreword

In Judges 6 we read the account of an angel of the Lord appearing to Gideon, whilst he threshed wheat inside a wine-press. The angels declaration astonished Gideon, for he declared "The Lord is with you, you mighty man of valor!" Gideon is hiding in a winepress for fear of the Midianites. No one would blame young Gideon for looking around to see who else was in the winepress, because as we read on his view and perspective of himself was nothing like the way the Lord saw him. "I am the least" meaning the weakest, is the way he saw himself. Yet, the Lord saw him as a mighty man of valor and perfect for the task.

The Lord is God, so He cannot be wrong - ever! It wasn't the Lords perspective that was wrong, but the perspective of Gideon that had to be realigned to match the Lords. Without a change in his viewpoint, Gideon would never be able to fulfil the call of God over His life.

In Matthew 16:13, we read of when Jesus asked Peter "Who do men say I am?" Peter listed what some people were saying about Jesus. But then Jesus asked Peter directly, "But who do you say I am." I know for sure Jesus didn't ask Peter this question because He was in a moment of doubt or insecurity and needed encouragement. He was testing Peters perspective, his vision, his lens. Was he able to see Jesus as He really was, or through the natural lens of man. When Peter announces that Jesus is "the Christ, the Son of the living God." Immediately Jesus knew Peter could only perceive and 'see' this, because his optics had been changed to see from the Fathers perspective. He wasn't seeing the Jesus of Nazareth, the carpenters boy. Peter absolutely knew Jesus was the long awaited Messiah and Son of God.

In this wonderfully written book, "The Lens Of The Father," Dennis unfolds the truths that he learned on his own personal journey of healing and deliverance, to see the painful and tragic events of his life through the lens of the Father. The result was, and is, a glorious account of Fathers lavish grace of changing Dennis' lens, to see the events in such a new, unimaginable way, that it turned what the Devil meant for bad, into the victory and liberty of the Holy Spirit in Dennis' life.

Dennis tenderly walks you through his journey with such honesty and openness which is rare, inviting us all to take the same journey of healing and deliverance from the scars received in our walk, by gaining the Lens of the Father. I promise you, he will guide you with wisdom beyond years, that he gained from Father along the way.

To say he experienced a life changing encounter with Father, is not just catchy words, but is true. He was transformed into a different man when his perspective was changed.

Are you ready for your life to change? You are! Then take his hand and let him lead you into the realms of Father's love and grace that just maybe, you never understood were waiting for you all this time. Be brave. Believe!

Wynne Goss

Chapter One

My "HIS" Story

I want to share some of my story, and I hope and pray it will bless someone who has struggled on different levels as I have. For me, the struggle was primarily because I wondered why God had allowed some of the things I had experienced in life. The words that I share in this book come from a place deep within my inner being, realized after many sessions of therapy, time in prayer, and countless conversations.

I have realized over the years how important it is to keep my heart open and my mind renewed to receive new information about my life which could become supplementary branches of awareness. These new branches of awareness continue to provide the Holy Spirit greater access to my soul so healing can reach every part of my being. I want to be vulnerable but clear at the same time. It can be scary and even formidable to open your heart after trauma or pain of any kind. As a believer in the Lord Jesus, I understand vulnerability will cause fear to evaporate like water landing on hot pavement in the heat of summer.

Speaking as a person who has experienced trauma and pain at different places in my life, I'm honestly certain I have caused others pain even if it was not my true intention. I know how critical it is to have the right people in my life to hold me close as a friend, without judgement, especially when I can't find the language to put to the pain. I've had plenty of times in my life when I was too ashamed of my story. I was too full of guilt from weaknesses in my own flesh to share with others what my real issues were. I thought, even *believed*, for a long time that it was something wrong with me.

I've said so many times, I didn't have a clue how close the Lord was with me in everything that I was experiencing in my life. I'm so glad I decided to arrive at this place in my life, marriage, and ministry to finally share my story. We all have a story to tell, and it's important that we learn from our experiences before we tell our story. This way healing, restoration, and the knowledge we gain isn't something we try to tell people about, it's something we get to share. We help others recognize the courage that's within them to become an overcomer.

When God created this world, He used words. When He created man, it was on the heels of a conversation with the Godhead. There's so much power that can be experienced in a conversation.

From a Natural Mother to a Spiritual Mother

My parents gave me to my grandparents to raise as their own child when I was just a baby. I had no idea as a child what the totality of this one decision would have on my entire life. This decision would in time also become the catalyst to align me with the plan the Lord would have for me as I got older.

I grew up always going to church with my grandmother. As a child, it felt like it was almost every other day. But my grandfather never came with us. At first it didn't register, but over time, I started to notice his absence whenever we went to church.

I began to see differences between the both of them. My grandmother would get up early and cook breakfast.

My grandfather would eat and leave for work, and I wouldn't see him until later that night. My grandmother would spend a lot of time in her room on her knees in prayer. As a child, I knew enough from the time I had spent in church listening to sermons that something wasn't right. I just didn't know what it was.

I went about doing the things that children do. As I got a little older, but still a child, I can remember my grandfather telling my grandmother that he was going to start taking me with him whenever he left the house. I can remember (to some degree at least) that she wasn't happy with his decision to start taking me with him. It wasn't anything that she said; it was simply the way that she looked. From the time she and I spent together even as a child, I could sense something, but I didn't know what I was sensing or what it meant.

When you're a child under the age of ten and your grandfather wants to take you with him in his truck, it's exciting. It almost feels like you're getting an opportunity to spend time with a genuine hero. There's something magical about grandparents in the eyes of a child. They seem larger than life. I'm sure it has a lot to do with having reared their own children and getting another chance to correct the mistakes they had made.

As I look back at that very moment when I first rode with my grandfather, I was filled with sheer excitement as the adrenalin rush made my heart race. I wondered what places we would explore and adventures we would have together. These feelings seemed to override whatever expression my grandmother had on her face. In the eyes of a small child, my grandfather and a big truck was the ultimate time spent. I was just a child, but in my mind, I had somehow passed a test. It was time to move to the next phase in the growing up process, and I was ready.

As I ran to the truck, mind racing, all I could think about were the things that I'd be able to share with my friends at school, and they would be awesome! When my grandfather and I pulled out of the driveway, I immediately wanted to roll the window down so I could feel the force of the wind pushing against my hand.

After driving for a while, we pulled into a neighborhood and stopped at a house where we got out of the truck and walked toward the front door. We were greeted by a lady who I didn't know and had not seen before. I could tell by the way my grandfather walked in that he knew her, and she knew him. It somewhat reminded me of the expression on my grandmother's face before we left. I couldn't put my finger on it at the time, but things felt different. We stayed for a while, but no other kids came in the room with us, so I was unsure why we were at this house with this strange lady.

After some time passed, we prepared to leave. My grandfather didn't say anything about why we were at a house with this lady I didn't know, and I didn't ask. I had a feeling that I didn't have language for at the time. I had never felt like this before. I didn't know what it was, and I didn't know what to do with it.

It was a long and quiet trip home. My grandfather didn't say anything, and I didn't either. As a child, I didn't really know what to say or think about this situation. When we got closer to home, I started to think about what questions my grandmother might ask when we got back. I had no idea what I'd say; I had no answers. I also began to wonder if this was the reason why my grandmother had that look on her face before we left, that look which seemed to convey a feeling that she wasn't pleased with my grandfather's invitation to me for a ride along.

However, once we arrived home, we were greeted as though everything was normal. My grandmother didn't ask questions, and my grandfather didn't say anything about where he had taken me or who the strange lady was. As it got closer to bedtime, I really started to wonder what was taking my grandmother so long to ask me questions. It seemed like that night was the longest night of my life. The next morning came, and I thought surely she'd ask at the breakfast table.

She didn't ask anything, and they just went about the day as usual, as if everything was fine. Unfortunately, when I arrived home from school, it started all over again when my grandfather said, "Let's go."

I thought there'd be no way my grandmother would let me go again without saying something, but there were no words spoken. I got in the truck with much less enthusiasm than the day before, thinking I didn't want to get my hopes up in case we were to end up at the same place again. Then I thought there's no way it was a one-time thing, but I tried to convince myself my grandparents had worked things out when I was in school. As a child, that's what you tell yourself when you don't understand grown-up issues.

I was wrong! We ended up at the same house with the same woman, but this time she and my grandfather seemed a lot more comfortable with each other. I was allowed to go outside and play while my grandfather visited this woman. I remember a brick-enclosed goldfish pond in her back yard that seemed mysterious to me, mainly because I hadn't seen a small fishpond in anyone's backyard before.

This was the second time visiting this house, but it would become part of a regular routine for years. Over time, the feelings I'd had at first which I couldn't originally put into words became very clear. It was anger! I hated going to her house. The visits to her home soon turned into trips to the lake and out of town, and I started to think this was like having another family.

My grandfather had another woman in his life, and that was just the tip of the proverbial iceberg. When he was home with us, he was kind. I never heard or noticed any arguments between him and my grandmother. They never even seemed to be visibly upset with each other. None of it really made sense to me growing up.

One of the many things that stood out while growing up and spending time with him and this other lady was when he got me my first bicycle. He took it over to her house for me to ride it. I was very conflicted about this. I had excitement over the bike, but wondered why my grandmother couldn't see me riding it for the first time.

The Two Realities

I lived in two very different worlds. When I was with my grandmother in our home, I was at peace and felt like everything was fine. On the other hand, when I was with my grandfather, he took care of my needs, but I didn't have the same feelings of peace because I never liked the fact that he had another lady in his life who wasn't my grandmother. I also hated that he took me with him to see her. I didn't understand it all, but in some ways, I began to wonder if this was the reason why my grandmother spent so much time praying. Perhaps she hoped God would touch my grandfather's heart, and he would change?

The contradictory lifestyles my grandparents exposed me to were from two opposing extremes. The relationship my grandfather had with this lady went on from as early as I can remember. It continued until he died of a stomach ulcer before my 10th birthday. The relationship my grandmother had was with the Lord and was always strong. Everybody loved and respected her, at least that's what I remember and understood as a child.

In the case of my grandmother, it was always church, prayer, and talk of trusting in the Lord and believing that He would take care of things. On the other hand, my grandfather didn't seem to have interest in church or the Lord whatsoever. I never heard him pray, and we certainly didn't pray together like my grandmother had done for so long.

After my grandfather passed away, I remember asking my grandmother why she never said anything to him about what he was doing. I was angry and explained how I had never wanted to be with him or his lady friend at her house or on trips. My grandmother simply explained that she always put her cares in the hands of the Lord, and she trusted the Lord to fix them. I heard what she said, but I didn't understand it because she never said anything to him, at least not in my presence.

My grandfather's passing opened the door for me to start asking questions for the first time. I had a few questions to ask, and trust me when I say this, I had no idea what I was about to set in motion.

I asked her, "Why am I with you? I have a mother, a father, four brothers, and five sisters. Why am I with you?"

The answer came in the form of a story. When you

ask a question, and the first thing you get is a long pause followed by a story, you may need to sit down.

I was about fourteen at the time of this conversation. She said when my father was a baby, he was dropped off on her doorstep for her to raise. As my young ears heard the story, my body went into what I call spiritual paralysis. What?

In that moment, which felt like hours, I couldn't move, breathe, or hear anything else. In my mind, that meant this woman who had raised me was not my biological grandmother. I heard what she said, but my mind wondered how this could even be possible. I mean, how could it be that after growing up and spending fourteen years of my young life with someone I thought was my only grandmother, that she was no blood relation to me?

Once I came to myself, I realized I didn't want to just accept her word as the truth; I needed to corroborate her story. I told her I was going to see my mom and dad and talk to them about it. My mother and father and siblings lived in the same neighborhood but several blocks away. When I arrived at their house, I told my mother the story my grandmother had just shared. Without hesitation, she turned away from me and walked into her bedroom. She came back shortly after retrieving my birth certificate and gave it to me.

The moment I looked at my birth certificate, I immediately realized my surname was different than the name I had used in school for the last fourteen years. My mom didn't speak to my newfound discoveries, and it left me completely in a fog. I left the house with my birth certificate and headed back home, not really sure what I would say when I arrived.

Upon arriving back home, I just laid down and went to sleep. I had so many thoughts and feelings surrounding what the truth was. Who was I? It all seemed to happen so fast and was very hard to process. The one thing that I was clear on and never doubted despite this shocking news, was I knew my grandmother loved me unconditionally. That truth took me forward until I was able to get the help I needed to connect the dots of the trauma in my life.

I then began to wonder why I was here on this earth. That question took time to reveal. It would take the experiences of a failed marriage, pastoring one church and planting another, therapy, "heart healing" ministry sessions, and countless conversations with mentors where I would often end up crying in the fetal position. At times I even self-medicated. It was many years before I asked God for forgiveness so I could come to a place in my mind (and heart) to accept the Truth of my God-given identity.

I wanted to be vulnerable and share a portion of my story to provide foundational context as I write this book. I hope it will help you open your heart and mind to those uncomfortable crossroads in your life, and prompt you to get any necessary help needed to bring you peace. It is only when you speak from a place of restoration that you can help others. I'm not writing from a place of blame. This isn't about what happened to me; this is about what happened *for* me. I believe the painful things I've experienced have served me well. Of course, I didn't realize what the positive benefit would be at the time. I was hurting and cried like anyone else would while in the middle of a process not understood. I overcame. So will you. Thank you, Jesus!

Matthew 3:17 NKJV - *And suddenly a voice came from heaven, saying, "This is My beloved Son, in whom I am well pleased."*

Chapter Two

Hidden Nuggets

We all have a story to tell. I've found that typically our story begins with us, and then is shaped in the forefront of our minds. We tell ourselves that "my story is what it is," but during less hectic times, we begin to share those same realities and life experiences with others. The same is true for me. Eventually as we grow and mature in life, even as a teen or young adult, the more we share our story. This oftentimes leads to more questions surrounding who we really are or why we were born in the first place. It's these types of questions that led me to some major discoveries, some of which I want to share in this book.

What began as my story became my testimony over time. It highlights the type of things I experienced as a child growing up, and the hidden nuggets I discovered along the way as I connected the dots of my life's story. It was not easy nor was it a quick process in my journey of discovery. But eventually, the insights and revelations from the Holy Spirit would come together to transform my life.

As a leader, I've learned it has always been (and it still is) very important to be open and honest with myself and with others. I believe this is the best way for the Lord to maximize our capacity to love, serve, and simply "be" to the fullest extent possible. I have made mistakes along the way, and I'm sure I will make more as I continue to live on this earth. However, I will continue to learn and grow because of those mistakes.

I mentioned earlier that everyone has a story. The thing about our story is there are some influences due to our past experiences in life which may cause us to deviate in our minds from the truth when we share those events. It is essential to allow the Holy Spirit to reveal those areas that don't fully align with His Word and the Truth of who we really are.

One of the things that helped me in this approach was to utilize the tools I'd used in my inner heart healing sessions. It was recognizing that Jesus was with me in my story even when I couldn't sense him.

The moment I made up my mind to take another look at my past to learn instead of focusing on my pain, I started to see things a little bit clearer, and the nuggets in my story became visible. I didn't realize the role my emotions had played in preventing me from seeing things the way the Lord wanted me to see them.

It was through the Holy Spirit's wisdom, I began to discover that everything I thought was true in my story, was not necessarily pointing me toward my true identity. Without realizing it, I had begun to embrace some untruths. My mindset clung to these lies and began to embrace a false identity. I was living life from places where I had experienced pain instead of living from a place of strength where I should have been relinquishing those things to Jesus.

As a man, and especially as a leader in ministry, it was important for me to reflect and walk through my past with a mindset of discovering Truth and not just reliving the pain. The knowledge in these places of pain and limitations is what I needed to understand and grow from.

Once I surrendered to this important process of discovery, while posturing my heart to receive Truth, the Holy Spirit started highlighting my story in a significantly different way. He revealed that He not only wanted me to receive and live from that place of Truth in my identity in Christ, but how He wanted me to see how my healing and deliverance, coupled with the knowledge of what I'd learned, would bring greater insight into my story.

It was at this point that I really began to hear the gentleness of the Holy Spirit, who then led me to reevaluate my thought process. This time He wanted me to listen and look to the Holy Spirit for the hidden nuggets of revelation that would help me connect the dots of truth of my story. What was so phenomenal during this process, is that the hidden nuggets were in the exact same places where Jesus had healed my broken heart!

I knew my story. I had lived it, and I felt there really couldn't be that much left to uncover. Or was there? The Lord always knows what He's doing and why. Usually when we surrender to His will and purposes for our lives, this is when we are amazed by His love, grace, and mercy. So, I yielded to what I felt led to do, and as a result, I'm sitting down at a table writing! To me, my testimony was that powerful, and I believed it was what the Lord wanted me to do.

One of the biggest lessons I learned (or hidden nuggets I discovered) was regarding the limited mindset I had carried for so long. I had no clue how my life and my decisions, whether large or small, and how my mindset had been influenced by my parents giving me away as a baby. This was a huge hidden nugget to uncover! But the Lord began to very kindly say to me, "You're giving *My credit* and glory to your parents."

I had to pause for a moment before countering, "But Lord, this is what happened to me when I was a baby."

He then gently replied, "Son, you don't have the story correct."

The things God spoke into my heart next changed everything from that point on, but I'll start with this knowledge nugget. When I look back, I often said my parents gave me away. In my mind this was true. My perception was they didn't really want me because I wasn't that important.

However, when I began to examine the knowledge the Lord began to share with me, I could see His divine providence. For the first time, I could see the hand of the Lord orchestrating the plans He had for my life through everyone involved. I could also see how important it was for me to process my entire story moving forward in this same way, because knowledge is power.

At that moment, all I wanted to do was revisit my past to discover even more hidden nuggets of knowledge and truth. It became even more exciting as I started to discover small details which made a huge difference in the way I not only "saw" the events in my life, but in the way I shared this information with others.

The Lord began to speak to me in His still small voice in such a loving and caring way, as if I were still a young child. He said He was in charge of everything in my life. I could see how my parents were the instruments He had chosen to position me where He wanted me to be placed. This little pivot in my thinking helped me not only to understand and dig deeper into my story, but also to dig deeper into myself. In all transparency,

I had missed these things before because I was too focused on the pain, insecurity, limited thinking, and the unanswered questions.

The words of wisdom and knowledge the Lord began to share with me in those moments were so powerful. They were so clear and concise! No more skewed lens or foggy perceptions. This was a greater spiritual awakening for me as an adult, and it created a major shift in the way I saw myself. The greatest part was it transformed the way I listened to others as they also shared their past traumas. It enhanced the way I was able to receive from the Lord, too. Once I had experienced the healing power of the Father as well as His delivering grace, Romans 8:28 came alive in my heart. I knew all these things had been working together for my good all along! The knowledge that He was pouring out was not just saturating my heart and increasing my love for my heavenly Father, it was allowing me to embrace the real and authentic me.

I also began to understand that I could no longer focus solely on healing because you can be healed without understanding what the Lord wants you to learn. It's this revelation and knowledge of my story which will make the greatest impact on this world. I didn't realize when I was healed that I also needed to *learn* from my process. I came to understand I could no longer have just the faith that He would bring me through it, I would also need to trust God fully to teach me during the process.

I really didn't understand at first why the Lord wanted me to revisit my story, and quite honestly, I wasn't excited about diving into this process. Now, I'm so glad I did. Otherwise, I would not have discovered the hidden nuggets God had planned for me. I wanted to learn everything He wanted me to learn. I want everyone to know what God desires them to know about their own undiscovered stories. It's important to share your experiences with His Truth and perspective. Now, I want you to discover the hidden nuggets of YOUR story. It's become my passion to write. That's all because I revisited my past and uncovered the hidden nuggets which Holy Spirit wanted me to know.

I didn't have a clue just how much I needed to learn from my past. My focus was primarily on heart healing. I told my story from the place I experienced the pain, but that was *my* truth and not *His* Truth. The Lord began doing a story makeover for me. Let Him do the same for you!

The Lord has a plan for all of us. When He has a plan for your life, I can say with certainty it will come with some pain along the way. It's always good to have people in your life who are loving and trustworthy to support you as you revisit your past. As you arrive at a place where you can surrender and allow the Holy Spirit to heal your heart and discover revelation about what you've gone through, you will ultimately grow both spiritually and emotionally. This will also lead you to the purpose that God has for your life.

I was able to discover what I had not been able to see before. This kept me from seeing me as a complete person in Christ. This is the "why" behind why the Lord wanted me to revisit my past to gain the knowledge He wanted to impart to me as a son. He knew that I still had times where I didn't fully embrace my position as His son. The Lord always knows why He does what He does… it's up to us to trust Him with our hearts.

The first step we take in an act of obedience is always the most important one to take. That step for me was my story. I realized the Lord wanted to teach me more than what I didn't know, He wanted me to get closer to Him as a son.

As I grew up in my grandparents' home, and even as an adult, I had initially viewed my life in such limited ways. I had allowed my broken heart to be my instructor. I was clueless regarding how it was forming a belief system that was soul-destroying. Anytime the heart takes the lead, most of your story processing will be from an emotional place. The thing about your emotions is they can be up or down and all over the place, especially when the pain of trauma has not been dealt with.

I was able to make an extreme pivot, starting at the very beginning when I recognized the Lord in His rightful position of authority in my story. We can have faith in the Lord and still not have the knowledge of what we've gone through in life from a spiritual perspective. This can result in a lack of authority as a son of God because the knowledge hasn't opened to us.

The more this knowledge settled in my spirit, the more I renewed my mind from that place, and the more secure I became in my walk with the Lord. I finally accepted that the difficult things in my life happened *for* me and not *to* me. This profession of faith and Truth empowered me. It truly helped me stay in my Kingdom position, postured with the heart of a true son of God created in His image.

Ephesians 1:5 NKJV ...*having predestined us to adoption as sons by Jesus Christ to Himself, according to the good pleasure of His will.*

Chapter Three

Truth vs. Fact

I have been intentional and transparent while sharing my story. It is with the sincerest hope that it will cause you to take another look at your story through the eyes of Christ. I've come to realize that in many cases we can gain more knowledge and insight, but when any knowledge is still on an earthly level, it doesn't provide us with the vision Christ wants for us. My goal is to use my testimony as a tool that will assist you spiritually and emotionally, much like how the clay on the potter's wheel is formed by the touch of the potter's hands and the turning of the wheel. We can all benefit from the constant turning and reshaping process of life until our true form and purpose is revealed.

My story may not be too surprising to some, but to others, it may seem unimaginable. However, we all have a common thread that we share... we all have a story. And your story, like mine, is worth revisiting in a manner where the Holy Spirit can be the narrator in Truth instead of the pain that may have taken center stage of our past history. Truth will also extinguish the opinions of others.

From the moment I was obedient to the Lord to revisit my past through His eyes, what really stood out to me was how I had allowed pain to be the main character. I didn't realize just how fully I had embraced the victim mentality. I didn't just incorporate pain in my conversations about my past, it became my badge of honor.

This was a light bulb moment for me. I truly began to see and understand why the Holy Spirit was compelling me to write. My understanding of pain and rejection started very early. As a child, I thought because I was given away, I wasn't good enough. Then when family withheld knowledge of what really happened, I was left to create my own thoughts and belief system.

The Lord never intended me to feel pain, rejection, or to have a limited perception of myself or Him. According to NKJV, Proverbs 22:6, *"Train up a child in the way he should go, And when he is old he will not depart from it."* I can't stress the importance of this passage of scripture and the necessity of starting the training process as soon as possible with children.

I was trained to have faith in the Lord, but I wasn't taught that the pain I had experienced in my life didn't belong to me. Subsequently, I took ownership of the pain. Then because I took possession of something that didn't belong to me and didn't come from the Lord, I began giving the enemy access to my heart, will, and emotions.

I saw my life growing up through pain (or the orphan heart), and not through the love of God. This led to self-reliance and a poverty mindset. The enemy capitalized on my pain because it was real to me; it was a "fact." The enemy knew if he could get me to focus on my pain, it would eventually cause me to have negative thoughts. Then those thoughts, if not met with Truth, would be the basis of my belief system. That's why it's critical to understand Truth early in life, to prevent you from becoming a victim!

After receiving God's Truth that I am more than a conqueror, I began to embrace that I wasn't responsible for the actions of others. Therefore, the pain that I experienced did not belong to me. The more I accepted this new mindset, the more I realized it didn't matter that I was given away. It became less significant to focus on having been rejected. It just did not matter because I knew the feelings and mindset which had stemmed from those facts never were mine to carry.

I had taken on something that started early in my life, but none of the pain and dysfunction ever belonged to me or my family. By God's grace and mercy, I came to understand I needed to become knowledgeable regarding how my experiences were affecting my personal relationship with my heavenly Father. The moment I began to see how I had created an ungodly perspective from the pain, it became very clear that the mind of Christ was what I not only wanted, but needed, in order to experience true freedom.

To be clear, it wasn't that my heart wasn't hurting. It was, indeed. It's just that when we accept it's not our burden to carry, we can release those burdens to our heavenly Father, for He cares for us. As a matter of fact, He never intended for us to experience the pain. That's the truth!

This is what I call the breakthrough! It's the moment where you recognize that what and how you've been believing is false. It is only when you receive the Truth of the Lord that you can change your mind to simply receive it and embrace His Truth.

The Truth of the Kingdom of God is not the same as the truth that we get from the facts of this world. Yes, we live in a fallen world, but we don't have to remain in a fallen state of mind. Truth resonates in these words of Jesus, "I have come that they may have life, and that they may have it more abundantly." If you only believe worldly facts, they will cause you to think there's no hope, and you may as well give up. The Truth of the Kingdom does not focus on the condition of this world, it focuses on Jesus as the solution. He is the way, the Truth, and the life! Abundant life can be found and experienced in Jesus.

The moment I changed my mind, stopped living with a victim mindset, and received the Truth of the Kingdom, I realized that victory was always mine. I didn't have to earn it because it was already purchased by Jesus on the cross for you and me. That is what made all the difference in my life, and it can make all the difference in your life as well!

It was through this transformed mind that I was able to truly receive everything that Jesus had for me. It became easier to reject the old mindset and cast down vain imaginations connected to limitation, poverty, and the orphan's heart. It's also very important to stay connected to like-minded believers who will tell you the Truth and not just recycle worldly facts and negative beliefs. Worldly facts are connected to the earthly realm, where Kingdom Truth is directly from God. As believers in Christ, the Truth is linked to: *"whatsoever is pure, whatsoever is lovely and a good report."* The truth is that He's a kind Father, full of love and compassion.

The enemy uses our lack of knowledge more than anything else to deceive us into thinking and feeling in ways which are against the Word of God. He does it with facts instead of Truth. The facts may cause you to interrogate the Lord without you even knowing it because facts are tangible. We must always remember the Truth of the Lord stands above the facts of the world.

The facts of my life were real, but the Lord wanted me to realize His Truth has more power than anything of this world. The Lord was not the One who caused me to experience what I did in life, but the Truth of His Word caused things to work together for my good. Romans 8:28 is evidence in my life in that, *"all things work together for good."* It will do the same for you.

The thing about our heavenly Father is that even though bad things can happen in our lives, He can cause those things to turn around for our good. There's a higher purpose, there's a greater good. I want my story of truth to be evidence of that fact no matter how difficult life's challenges have been. The Lord gives us all freewill to make our own choices, so the beginning of our growth process is when we take ownership of our life and stop blaming others for things that happened in it.

Galatians 4:6 NKJV - *And because you are sons, God has sent forth the Spirit of His Son into your hearts, crying out, "Abba, Father!"*

Chapter Four

Through a Child's Eyes

As a child, I started to realize that I didn't have a clue regarding all the different ways I would be impacted by the decisions which were made for me. It's not always the norm for families to have a father, mother, and siblings growing together and sharing life's memories under the same roof. It certainly wasn't the case for me. However, it was never the plan of our heavenly Father for families to be separated or broken in any way. Brokenness in families contributes to so many dysfunctional places in our society which can all be traced back to the family.

One of the things that was a saving grace for me was my grandmother, who was Spirit filled and had devoted her entire life to Christ. She was the catalyst that introduced me to Christ at an early age, and for that, I will forever be grateful.

I received Christ when I was a child. And when I look back as an adult, I can better understand why at times I struggled to receive the love of Christ. It was because I wasn't taught that Jesus did more than forgive sin, He also healed hearts from the brokenness caused by a lack of knowledge.

The enemy capitalized on the decision my parents made regarding who would raise me. He took advantage of that decision by planting thoughts in my mind as a child in a manner that blocked my capacity to receive. Actually, I didn't know how to believe or receive the Truth. However, I want to make it very clear: the enemy is a liar, and he was defeated at the cross by Jesus. But even though he was defeated at Calvary, he's still a deceiver and manipulator of situations that have the potential to cause us to think in ways that are completely false.

In my situation, when I was given to my grandmother, she was not aware of how the enemy would use it to not only keep me in bondage, but also to tear my family apart. This is why the scriptures tell us in Philippians 2:5, *"Let this mind be in you which was also in Christ Jesus."* Jesus had compassion, but never allowed His emotions to take the lead in His life. When we have the mind of Christ, we process things through the Spirit of God and don't allow the enemy to have control of our emotions and thoughts to gain an advantage.

Like most of us, I had to mature to a place where I could allow the Holy Spirit to transform my mind so that I could overcome the orphan heart and mindset. The orphan mindset partners with pain. When it does, it can easily cause you to feel rejected, unwanted, and/or unloved. These were thoughts that I had as I grew up. I really believed they were true. I didn't have a clue that the enemy was using the pain I felt as leverage to deceive me. The evidence became very clear to me. The more I allowed the Holy Spirit to dismantle my thoughts of feeling blame or being unworthy, the more I could see and know the Truth. It was one thing to separate fact from truth in my story, however, it was an entirely new spiritual level that the Holy Spirit invited me to experience. In essence, He encouraged me to release the blame on anyone for the way I had felt for so long and to receive the Father's love and Truth.

The Lord has a wonderful plan for everyone, and it doesn't include pain and heartache. This is something

I want to talk about more in depth in the next chapter. Simply put, the pain and heartache that we may experience in life comes from our own decisions and our own lack of knowledge.

The Lord is a kind and loving Father. He has given us free will to make our own choices in life. He doesn't force us to come to Him, nor does He do things that make things hard for us; that's just not in His nature. He does, however, give us power to overcome the enemy. By renewing our minds and seeing God's Truth by faith, it becomes easier to yield our will to Him when we find ourselves in challenging or hurtful places.

There were so many times when I thought I was broken and honestly believed I could fix myself if I only tried hard enough. The real truth was I wasn't broken at all. The feelings that I had were real because I could feel pain, but the origin of my pain was generated by the questions the enemy wanted me to pose in my mind. The one thing that the enemy uses to promote his plan is deception! The moment we give our attention to the voice of the enemy, deception moves in, and we come in agreement with the enemy (oftentimes without even knowing it). The deception is the lie. I spent way too much time focusing on the details instead of the things the Lord wanted to reveal. His desire was that I could see (and embrace) the Truth... God's Truth.

I have learned over time it's not the lie I need to correct. It's my response to the enemy's tactics that needs to change. When I can better recognize the point of origin where the deception begins, I won't even engage the enemy, and as a result, the lie will never materialize. Then and only then will I maintain the victory that Christ established on the cross.

The more I began to receive and embrace my true identity as a son of God, the more I realized that pain was never meant for me. Then it became even more critical for me to renew my mind. The renewing of my mind meant everything. Here's the reason why. It's the process of moving forward with the knowledge to overcome worldly "facts" and live in the Truth of the Word of God. The Lord would remind me from time to time that it wasn't just the pain, it was the way the enemy wanted me to think about the pain. That was the moment that I was not only restored in my spiritual sight, but I realized that my mindset was just as important in my process. It was in this process that I learned how to be an even more effective vessel for the Holy Spirit to use. Through my pain and experience, I could then touch other people's hearts and bring restoration to their lives.

Another huge lesson in all this for me as the truth in my story was revealed, was not to be hard on myself for not catching the revelation of Truth sooner. I'll never forget the things I did because of the pain I felt in my own heart. It's through these things I've been enlightened in Truth and sight in the supernatural which will cause me to handle others with even more care as I share knowledge with them concerning their stories.

In the past, I became angry when I reflected on the times that I rode with my grandfather to see another woman, only to return home to a grandmother who treated him as though nothing was wrong. My old mindset was dominated by my emotions which left me hurt and upset. But now, instead of being agitated and angry at my grandfather, I realize this situation had never belonged to me, and therefore didn't warrant my emotional attention. The great news is that when you stay in your own emotional lane, there's no negative impact. This way, the enemy doesn't have an opening or access to your soul to manipulate the situation to cause you to have thoughts that are not connected to God's Truth.

I learned a very powerful lesson from my situation. The life we have is a gift. If we allow people, places, and things to cause us to think otherwise, we will blame others and become bitter. My grandmother's heart toward my grandfather remained consistent, and regardless of what he did, her faith never wavered. When I was a child, I didn't really understand how she could treat him as though he had done nothing wrong. This was the case even though he was more committed to someone else than he was to her.

Although things were once foggy to me as a child, I've now gained the wisdom of Christ, and the Truth about my identity is now crystal clear. I can see now that I should have taken a different perspective as I grew in the things of the Lord. It was not my problem to fix or my burden to carry. It didn't belong to me in any way, and I didn't understand that as a child. Back then, I wanted to fix everything, and that was a false burden that I carried. What's interesting is the fact that I didn't even know I was doing this.

I was able to witness as a child what I rarely see as an adult today. My grandmother's level of commitment to her marriage was unbreakable, even if it was to someone who had a total disregard for the institution of marriage and had a total lack of understanding of holy covenant. The more I look at my past through the eyes of Christ, the more I can see it was the grace and love of Christ that my grandmother clearly understood.

The authority and power of God is what was missing. It would have been amazing if my grandmother had simply used the power of her voice. However, this was not my responsibility, nor was it a part of my process. It was hers to learn within her own relationship with the Father.

From what I can remember as a child, the confrontations she had were always in love and Truth. Thankfully, my grandfather was never mean to my grandmother. He just had a very stubborn way and seemed to be unwilling to change, regardless of the love she expressed toward him. As a child, I felt like she should have gotten really angry and put him in his place. But I was a child, and I thought like a child. The thing I didn't realize at the time is that you can't force or manipulate people to change their will because you feel they should. It takes the Holy Spirit working in their hearts to facilitate change.

The impression my grandmother made on me as a child was very powerful, despite the fact that I didn't agree with how she handled my grandfather's continuous indiscretion. Based on what I do remember, she was steadfast, kind, and unmovable in demonstrating the love of God at all times. I have to be honest and say that I never witnessed my grandmother ever losing her cool. She was always calm and prayerful. When she spoke, her words were always saturated with God's love and kindness. The things that others couldn't see that she demonstrated, I had a front row seat to be able to witness myself.

I can also honestly say that when I was a child, I didn't adapt well to all the things that my grandmother taught me. I certainly didn't understand the unwavering grace she extended at all times. However, as I matured in the things of God, I began to understand the importance of what she had taught me. I was especially appreciative of this knowledge when I started to serve as a pastor. Through her example, I witnessed how to be calm and rely on the Holy Spirit in every situation.

Now that I have grown naturally and have matured spiritually, I look back at my story through the eyes of Christ instead of a lens of pain. I can also admit I really didn't know how to be a brother. I didn't know how to share at all, and a lot of family moments were wasted, surrendered to dysfunction. Those times could have been better spent laughing and creating better memorable moments together. As a result of how I felt, I spent my time trying to fit in everywhere, when in reality, I was born to stand out.

I can't emphasize just how important it was for me to actually realize the power in my story. All I needed to do was surrender to the Holy Spirit and allow Him to direct my focus to me instead of others.

I thought a lot about my grandfather during the time we spent together growing up before he passed. Basically, his lifestyle consumed the majority of my focus, and I wanted things to be different. The problem with the way I viewed him was it completely blocked me from giving any type of accountability to my grandmother. In my eyes, she was the one who was completely innocent. Or was she?

I had to take a closer look at my grandmother as I got older. Even though her commitment to my grandfather was solid, her lack of communication was the one thing that grabbed my attention as I got older. The entire time I grew up, I never witnessed her engage my grandfather in any way. What she always told me was to "always keep the peace." Not addressing issues was her way of maintaining harmony in her home. Now I'm all about keeping the peace, but there are times that warrant confrontation. When we talk about the things that bother us, regardless of how difficult we may think they are, it keeps the enemy from taking advantage of the situation. He can't gain a stronghold by causing us to judge others unfairly or by perceiving the Truth inaccurately when we are open and honest about the things that trouble us.

When my grandmother never questioned my grandfather or even struck up a conversation, the enemy easily deceived me into thinking it was fine not to talk about feelings. I know now unequivocally, that is not true. When we don't talk about things that bother us, it can easily cause us to feel resentment, and there's nothing good about resentment. I wasn't aware of it at the time, but that's actually what was happening to me because no one was talking to me about anything.

I've always respected and admired my grandmother's commitment to the Lord and devotion to my grandfather. However, I have to say I've often wondered what things might have changed if she had confronted him in love.

I have pastored two churches over the past 20+ years, and one thing that stands head and shoulders above everything else is communication. Words are very powerful according to Proverbs 18:21 (NIV): *"The tongue has the power of life and death."* When the Father began creation, there wasn't a reference of any kind. He simply (and powerfully) used words to form the world we live in today. The right words coming out of the mouth of a person with a gentle heart can cause people to hear the heart of the Father. It helps the person embrace Truth and trust God with their entire life. At the same time, the wrong words coming out of the mouth of a person with ill intentions can cause destruction.

When it came to my grandmother and grandfather, I was never hurt by the words they spoke to each other. They always interacted with one another in a cordial manner. I formed my perspective from words that were never spoken. It was their actions that formed my perspective (and mindset) about them and about life in general.

1 John 3:1 NKJV - *Behold what manner of love the Father has bestowed on us, that we should be called children of God!*

Chapter Five

The Orphan Heart

An orphan is a child who is deprived of at least one, but typically both parents through their deaths. It's not only defined in the natural, but also in the supernatural. This is a subject that has touched everyone at some point in their lives. This is a topic I want to sound the alarm on, especially when I discovered the spiritual impact it had on me! It would take another book to dive more deeply into the traits connected to the orphan heart and mindset. For now, I just want to share highlights in this chapter.

The orphan heart has affected me so much over the course of my life. In fact, it limited me from believing the Truth of who God says I am. So, I want to use this chapter to expose some of the ways it has influenced my heart and mindset. As I begin to share with you my story, you will hopefully be able to clearly recognize the orphan spirit when it happens in your own life.

The orphan spirit is a spirit which targets your heart and mindset. Its sole objective is to cause you to focus on living life independently of others. This results in doubting God's provision and protection. Basically, it causes fear about the future and ultimately hinders your covenant relationship with your heavenly Father. For years, I had no idea an orphan mindset was influencing my heart. Had I known, I would have broken that internal mindset long before I did.

The orphan spirit is a demonic spirit which belongs to the enemy. It is a very destructive spirit that hides in plain sight: when you experience a loss in the family, a rejection, an abuse of any kind, feelings of despair, a divorce, or anything connected to your emotions or trauma. It doesn't matter if you have a family or not. The enemy is always hunting for those that are vulnerable according to 1 Peter 5:8 (NIV): *"Be alert and of sober mind. Your enemy the devil prowls around like a roaring lion looking for someone to devour."* When you read this verse, it may sound scary, but it's the Truth. Our adversary doesn't play by any rules. He is always searching for those who will allow him an opening, especially for those lacking the knowledge to combat this spirit with Truth. The enemy will leverage this orphan mindset to create diabolical partnerships with the spirits of religion, fear, or pride to keep you from embracing the Truth of God's Word and who you are as God's child.

The enemy also has the same approach today as he did in the garden; he uses alluring questions to tempt God's children. Questions cause hesitation, and this results in doubting the authenticity and faithfulness of God. The enemy's objective does not change. It has been (and still is) a destructive trifold methodology according to the scripture in John 10:10a (AMP*): "The thief comes only in order to steal and kill and destroy."* The orphan mindset (heart) manifests in how we feel, think, and react to matters of the heart. If this false mindset goes undetected as we grow in the natural, it can easily mature spiritually into our belief system. When it starts affecting our faith, it will cause us to accept and live life heavily influenced by ungodly beliefs contrary to the Holy Spirit of Truth.

It happened to me. It's something that every other human has experienced. Some born-again Christians still experience this in their lives but are unable to identify it. The reason it impacts all of us is due to its origin in the Garden of Eden. When the enemy enticed Eve to eat of the "tree of knowledge of good and evil," it caused mankind to sever our Holy Covenant with God. Ultimately, this was the enemy's first attempt to steal God's provision and protection from us. Fortunately, it was only partially successful.

Often, the things that happen to us in our youth, the things that in our world are "normal," trigger beliefs of acceptance regarding our situation, even if those beliefs don't align with the Truth of God's Word. Then we ingrain our flawed belief system into our heart, and it becomes our sense of truth as we journey through life. In my situation, it started with my mother and father giving my grandparents full custody to rear me as their own. So, reflecting on the spiritual dynamics of being *"born into sin and shaped in iniquity"* (Psalm 51:5), then marrying this with my family dynamics, it was the perfect spiritual storm to keep me in bondage to the orphan heart.

As mentioned earlier, the enemy is always seeking whom he may devour, and my emotional journey afforded him the opportunity to further sow the seeds of discord in my family. I've learned through life experience that silence, especially on important issues, will always breed confusion and dysfunction. In this case, the dysfunction in my family made it easy for the seeds the enemy had planted to grow and produce pain and the orphan mindset.

As a child, I thought it was normal to feel the way I did. After all, no one even mentioned the word orphan in any conversation. The reason why I was with my grandparents was never discussed. (Remember, it wasn't until around age fourteen when I had a conversation with my grandmother that I discovered that we didn't share DNA.) I was reeling because I was the only child from my immediate family who was living with my grandparents. So, when I discovered that we were not blood related, my heart exploded with new unexplainable emotions. Quite transparently, I didn't even have language to describe those feelings.

At that time, I had no idea what was coming to the surface and what was being exposed. It was years later before I would be able to connect the dots in that moment and wrap my mind around the idea that my family was divergent from the norm, especially regarding my grandmother.

After time, I came to realize that I had been influenced by an orphan spirit throughout my youth and even into my adult life. As a result, my heart had been manipulated and my thoughts altered without me even knowing it. As previously mentioned, it was years later when I was able to connect the spiritual dots of the networking capabilities of the orphan spirit. I can't emphasize this enough. It is extremely important to begin to recognize this mindset's influence and expose it despite it being camouflaged as normal. It engrafted into every area of life. It crippled my capacity to even "receive" the *"Spirit of adoption, whereby we cry Abba, Father"* as a son of God (Romans 8:15 KJV).

It's not God's design or plan for you to think that pain and heartache are normal; it's not! The orphan heart doesn't discriminate. The enemy will take advantage of any situation to influence how you feel, think, and ultimately believe God as your provider and protector. Fear is a liar. It is the fruit of an orphan mindset. The fall of Adam and Eve in the Garden created a spiritual separation between humanity and God. The enemy wants everyone to believe the Father is really angry with us, and He wants to punish us. That's just simply not true. The enemy's plan is strategic. He creates a plan of attack in advance of his approach. That's what I meant earlier when referencing how he plays the long game. The command the Father gave to Adam was to not eat of the tree of knowledge according to Genesis 2:16-17 (AMP): *"¹⁶And the Lord God commanded the man, saying, 'You may freely (unconditionally) eat [the fruit] from every tree of the garden; ¹⁷but [only] from the tree of the knowledge (recognition) of good and evil you shall not eat, otherwise on the day that you eat from it, you shall most certainly die [because of your disobedience].' "*

The plan to deceive was set in motion when the enemy initiated rebellion in Heaven and was kicked out. So, when he approached Eve, the goal was to take advantage of that moment to gain an upper hand with the orphan spirit. As previously stated, these are just a few highlights concerning the orphan mindset and how it will blind you from the Truth that will make you free. There is so much knowledge to be gained regarding the depth and level of impact that the orphan spirit can have on a person's life and how they live out their purpose. I encourage you to prayerfully seek guidance from the Holy Spirit on ways to identify and expose this spirit so that you can break the cycle.

I do indeed want to take a closer look at Adam and Eve in the Garden for just a moment to share some insight into how the orphan spirit hides in plain sight. In Genesis 3:10 (AMP) Adam said: *"I heard the sound of You [walking] in the garden, and I was afraid because I was naked; so I hid myself."* I find it very interesting Adam would make that type of statement since he had spent time in the presence of God. Why would he suddenly be so afraid to the point where he thought he needed to hide? Adam said he was afraid. This statement indicates a feeling or emotion. The orphan mindset leads you to be afraid. Fear, at best, influences your covenant relationship with God. At worst, it destroys your faith in God and your reliance on Him as your ultimate life-giving source. When the enemy first approached Eve, he used questions to create doubt. Cunningly, he knew this would result in both Adam's and Eve's sin against God.

When the enemy first approached Eve, he posed the questions in a way that caused her to doubt God's Word. That doubt led both her and Adam into sin. The moment I started to believe what the enemy was telling me as a child, it caused my heart to doubt. This affected my relationship with my family. Doubt will always connect to fear in a way that makes you think you're not loved or valued in a relationship. Not only that, it can oftentimes make you believe those who DO love you, will only ever love you conditionally, for what you can do for them. This is unlike our heavenly Father who loves unconditionally. The enemy's simple question caused Eve to ponder, "What if?" He wants every opportunity to sow seeds of doubt. It doesn't have to be huge… just a slight opening is all it takes to create doubt leading to sin. Sin is what causes a wedge in our relationship with the Lord. The sin Adam committed is what we focus on more than anything else. However, the break in relationship originated when the enemy posed questions causing Eve to doubt.

What I didn't know (actually, couldn't have known without someone sharing Truth with me), was how doubt, sin, and fear work together with the orphan spirit to affect the heart posture and mindset. I want to make sure I make a strong connection here when I mention Adam and how he was affected by the orphan spirit. It means death and breaking covenant with God. It was Adam's actions that caused him to fear and to try to hide from the Lord in the Garden. The orphan spirit always affects the heart. The enemy always wants to separate us from our heavenly Father. He desires this more than anything else because he knows that separation from the Father is death for us.

There was so much I needed to learn (and ultimately experience) regarding healing and true deliverance before I attempted to start on my story. Once you receive healing, you're able to live free of accusations, blame, shame, and pain. This freedom launched my way to engage with the Holy Spirit as I began to write my story. Once I acknowledged the existence of this orphan mindset and learned how it had influenced my life, those ungodly beliefs fled, and the pain lifted. I realized at that point that it didn't matter what people said or what they thought about me. The freedom I began to experience daily, along with my faith in God, is now unshakable! With this mindset, I recognized and understood the real value in revisiting my past from a pure heart, with a posture of not trying to fix things. It's the Truth of God that should border the canvas of our stories! Ultimately, you'll begin to not only believe God for provision and protection, but you'll wholeheartedly receive the Spirit of Adoption to see God as your loving and kind Father.

Chapter Six

Identity is Everything

I've taken a lot of time to intentionally and fully process my feelings before I started writing this book. I have also taken time to pray and thoroughly consider how to put language to my feelings. It's my passion to tell the truth with respect, accuracy, and story integrity. I want to clearly show how I felt, thought, and reacted to being given to my grandparents to raise me as their own child. The primary reason this book is so important is because we all have had experiences and beliefs which were factual. However in most cases, the Lord wants our stories to shift in perspective and mindset. For me, sharing my story has become a mandate from the Father to clearly communicate the process of transformation.

My life experiences and emotional posture were important enough that God led me back to gain spiritual insight. He is faithful. I attained spiritual discernment and wisdom when I surrendered my heart to His process. I looked through the lens of the Spirit, unencumbered by emotions. Then Jesus began to reveal the flawed perception of my story, family, and myself to me. He made it very clear that I could have handled many things differently. However, I learned during the process that I didn't have the right to take ownership of pain because pain doesn't belong to me. I also understood clearly that I shouldn't blame anyone, either. It was only then that my heart began to receive a fresh abundance of grace and mercy. It also allowed me to relinquish the limited belief system I had been living with my entire life. Specifically, it was a place of victimhood, but now I fully embrace the Truth that *"all things work together"* and are purposeful for my life in order to help others through my experiences.

There are certain events that occur in life which can easily leave a lasting impression in your memory bank. That is true regardless of the amount of time that passes. I had such a moment, which started with a question I pondered for fourteen years. I can remember the moment as if it were yesterday. I had no idea at the time the firestorm of reactions and not-so-positive responses I would ignite by asking what I believed was a simple question. It was the proverbial calm before the storm.

It was a normal day when I started a conversation with my grandmother. By this time, it had been a few years since my grandfather's passing. Although I had often thought about it, no one had ever said anything, so I didn't mention it either. But on that otherwise typical day in my life, I asked my grandmother how things had been for her when she had grown up. She joyfully shared several stories about the time spent and the closeness she'd had with her family.

I was fascinated by all the wonderful things she shared surrounding her childhood. The more she shared, the more I began to realize my story time of childhood adventures was very different since I was not raised with my siblings and parents. Then the question that had been birthing in my heart up until that moment made its way to my voice and penetrated the atmosphere. I asked my grandmother, "How did I come to live with you?"

It was a moment quickly engulfed by silence! I'm sure it was a brief period, but it seemed like an eternity before she began sharing about my father. She had literally walked outside and found him in a blanket on the front porch. There was no note, and none of their friends or acquaintances ever said anything about an abandoned baby, so she and my grandfather decided to raise him as their own child. As he got older, my grandparents shared how they had discovered him, and how he was not their biological son. She further explained that my father requested his first child be raised by them. My grandmother then further elaborated and said, "That's where you came into the picture. You were his first born, and that's how you ended up with us."

I listened intently but wondered why no one told me before then. I had so many other questions, and they all seemed to want to surface at the same time. I figured it best to also ask my mother about this and decided to do it right away. We lived in the same neighborhood, so it didn't take me long to arrive at her house. Once I arrived, my brothers and sisters were with my mom, and I shared the conversation I'd had with my grandmother. My mother became visibly upset and started sharing random facts about my father's childhood, facts that included information about his siblings who I had no knowledge of at the time.

I was at a loss for words. It seemed blatantly obvious that everyone knew about this except for me. My mom left the room temporarily, but when she returned, she handed me my birth certificate. Little did I know the type of emotional whirlwind I would be heading into when I looked it over. I knew I had the same last name as my grandparents, but when my eyes focused on the box that said "Mother's Name," no maiden name was listed. I cannot remember exactly how I felt, but it wasn't over. More shocking news came when I discovered the box where my father's name should have appeared... It had a line drawn through it. Yes, you read that correctly. There was no father's name listed on the birth certificate. I felt like a spy whose cover had been blown. Even more mind boggling was that everyone seemed to know except me. I started the walk back home. I had no words. I could not form any sentences to fully express my thoughts and feelings. I knew I needed time to process what had just taken place. And to think this all started with a simple question...

Once I arrived back home, it was too much to even attempt to talk about at the time. Saying I was overwhelmed is an understatement. When I walked into the house, my grandmother simply stared at me and waited for me to speak. When I finally began to share what had transpired, she hugged me tightly. It was as if to say, "I'm sorry" or "I got you." This time, as well as every other time I was upset as a child, she would always say without fail, "That's your mother and father, and they will always be your mother and father as long as they live." She spoke with God's love and compassion. Even though I didn't understand at the time how my grandmother could remain positive (especially when my mother was anything *but* positive), she always remained uplifting with my emotional ups and downs.

As I've matured, I am extremely grateful my grandmother remained uplifting and encouraging. If she had not, I know deep down I would have become very bitter over the years. Instead, I learned how to forgive. I struggled for so long with feelings of rejection. When I finally learned to release the pain to my heavenly Father, it became obvious that I desired God's truth more than the pain I had embraced. There had been many occasions in my youth when I tried to talk to my mother about being given away. This was always met with conflict. I could never figure it out. Oftentimes that conflict caused me to have a less-than-positive perception of my mother even when I didn't *want* to have those thoughts or feelings toward her. I'm so thankful my grandmother began to spend more time praying for me. Her prayers for God to open my heart to forgive and let go likely saved me from a dismal existence.

Another question heavy on my heart as a child was related to the fact that no one told me anything about who I was. Grandmother always focused on forgiveness. In hindsight, perhaps that was best for her to try to keep the peace. She was relentless in her faith. She was unwilling to give place to the enemy, and she never changed her stance on that topic. I learned the reason she never altered her position or responses to conflicts was because of her knowledge of Jesus Christ. Grandmother always knew there was more involved to being a Christian than having faith in Christ. It meant that she was a carrier of his image. This is what the scripture in Genesis 1:27 (NIV) says: *"So God created mankind in his own image, in the image of God he created them; male and female he created them."*

My grandmother didn't allow her personal feelings to get in the way. She recognized this season was a turning point in my life, so she certainly didn't allow my feelings to get in the way either. Certainly, the child within would not be able to comprehend this level of love and sacrifice, but thankfully I can now recognize how I would not have had the opportunity to be transformed into the person, the son of God by design that I am today. The faith my grandmother had in Christ was more than a moment in time where she confessed her faith. At that time, I really thought she was just being nice because that's just who she was. What I discovered was it's always about Truth. She focused completely on the image she had been created in from the beginning. I didn't have a clue as a teenager. It would become clear to me years later after having spent years in the ministry leading a congregation and journeying through life as a husband and father to three children. The thing that has become crystal clear to me now is my identity. My grandmother knew our place on earth in a family was important. However, she also knew that our position in Christ comes with more weight. That's what I believe she was teaching me all along. She always pointed me to Christ.

I now also recognize the importance of our acknowledging and embracing our spiritual identity in Christ. This Truth was so challenging to comprehend when the pain of rejection was so intense. That pain occupied the spotlight in my life. Grandmother trusted the Truth more than worldly facts. On the contrary, my focus was always on facts. This left me constantly asking questions and seeking answers. Grandmother knew the more I followed the facts, the more questions I would have. She knew this would hinder me in accepting the Truth. The Truth stands alone, rarely needing an explanation. She was confident in her identity, and she gave me the latitude to reach that place in my heart in my own time. This would be a place of total surrender and acceptance. As I mentioned earlier, it took me time to fully relinquish my whole heart and let go of the pain and rejection. I encourage you to seek Truth in Christ alone. The facts will remain, but your perspective and heart posture will change. It is well worth it!

In a lot of cases, I've observed that people sincerely believe in Christ, and they know in their hearts that He gave His life for them to be saved. However, they really don't comprehend what this means. Therefore, they don't fully experience the fullness of Christ. He wants to do more than forgive us of our sins. He wants us to become aware of the Truth that we are made in the image of the Father. He wants us to embrace the fact that we are God's beloved sons and daughters. We are not only image bearers, we carry His DNA on the earth.

Philippians 4:13 NKJV - *I can do all things through Christ who strengthens me.*

Chapter Seven

Breakthrough

Breakthrough (noun) is a sudden increase in knowledge, understanding, etc. It's an important discovery that happens after trying for a long time to understand or explain something.

I received Christ as a child, but I didn't clearly understand then what it meant to live my life from the perspective of my true identity as a son. I believed Jesus died on the cross for my sins, was buried, and in three days, He rose again. I thought I was solid on that part of the message of salvation. But the older I got, the more I began to realize that when Jesus gave His life on the cross, it was for the penalty of sin which separated me from the Father. The moment I accepted His ultimate sacrifice, by faith, I understood that I had been reconciled back to God and had access to develop a relationship with my Father. What I didn't understand fully was those same sins were blotted out completely by the finished work of Christ on the cross. How powerful is that to learn that my sins had been blotted out was as though I had never committed sin in the first place!

So, as a child who grew up in church, I was very accustomed to different types of services. Often the worship services lasted a while with lots of preaching, singing, and praising the Lord. But not understanding fully the completed work on the cross as a child, I not only had a narrow view of the magnitude of my salvation in Christ, but also could not comprehend what people meant when I heard the word "breakthrough." For me, breakthrough was an event where someone testified how the Lord had saved a family member or someone unemployed was blessed with a new job after being out of work. So, it wasn't until I had been pastoring for a while and started to connect with different ministries that I started to understand more about the fullness of the unconditional love of God and His heart toward me as a son.

It was somewhere around ten years of serving in pastoral capacity that the Holy Spirit began to increase my desire to pursue Him and to seek His presence. I can remember praying and fasting more. On numerous occasions, I started receiving prophetic words about books God desired for me to write. I heard the words spoken to me about writing, but they didn't penetrate, at least not right away. It was during this same season that a spirit-led connection began with FatherHeart Ministries.

We co-hosted a week-long gathering entitled *FatherHeart a School*. It was not the usual worship experience that I was accustomed to. It was an immersive encounter with the Holy Spirit for five full days, and the heart of the Father was revealed to me in such a tangible way. I was able to really experience breakthrough at another level and dimension in the Holy Spirit. While there was some instruction and brief messages from the leaders, there were no lengthy sermons. It was simply true worship and a time of soaking in His presence, a time to open the heart for the Holy Spirit to fill it with the heart of the Father.

While it is challenging to put language to my FatherHeart experience, I can say unequivocally that my breakthrough experience was life changing. It was not just an opportunity for testimony, it expanded my spiritual capacity to receive my heavenly Father's unconditional love and overwhelming blessings. The more I allowed myself to become vulnerable to receive the Holy Spirit's wisdom, He began to show me how to release my heart fully into His care. In an instant after yielding to the Holy Spirit, I was transformed in my mind and heart. It was like the Father had taken me by the hand and walked with me through places in my life that I perceived as painful and confusing. Yet, not only did the pain and confusion dissipate, He added so much clarity and revelation. I knew I would never be the same.

One of the key areas that The Holy Spirit revealed in this encounter was regarding my grandfather. He began to show me that he really did love me and my grandmother. What I learned in that moment by the Spirit was this revelatory truth: my grandfather's father had not shown him the love that he needed as a child. So, my grandfather had done what he thought was acceptable. My heart softened because I realized the love that God had for my grandfather was the same love He had for me. The only love my grandfather knew was what his father demonstrated to him throughout his childhood and young adult life. What was also so powerful in that encounter was that God didn't make excuses for my grandfather or the other woman he was involved with. He simply and lovingly revealed His heart toward us all.

Next, the Holy Spirit began to share more wisdom and insight regarding my grandmother. He pointed out that some people exhibit love differently. At times, the way my grandmother expressed love appeared as if she was weak or afraid. But I learned that wasn't the case. Then something phenomenal and revelatory happened. God asked me, "Do you know how much strength it takes for a woman to have to share their spouse and covenant partner with someone else?" In that moment, I was really able to see her through the eyes of Christ. I understood that she was more powerful than I even realized. She stood by her word, "For better or worse." I could not help wondering how much her love for me influenced her decision to stay. How much was I on her mind when she kept silent about her own pain?

The Father also reminded me that He doesn't force people to accept Him or His love. Everyone has a choice. I knew then that I had truly forgiven my grandfather. I also knew I had accepted the fact that he loved me. Anything that I didn't understand or was left unrevealed in that moment, I fully surrendered to the Father's care.

Now, I wanted to understand more about my earthly mother and father. I remained in God's presence and waited for Him to reveal what insight I needed. The Holy Spirit started to reveal how my father never had the blessings of knowing who his birth mother was nor who his natural father was. While another mother reared me, I was blessed to know both of my natural parents. This was something my father would never experience. Once again, my heart of compassion and the revelation of God's unconditional love overtook me. In that moment, I put myself in the place of my father who was dropped on someone's porch; he had been rejected by his birth mother and given to someone else to raise. The Father then paused for a moment…

The Holy Spirit then showed me my mother. He posed another thought-provoking question. "Have you placed one of your children in the arms of someone who you loved, who wasn't related to you, and asked them to raise your child?" I stopped in my spiritual tracks of this divine encounter. For the very first time in my life, I began to understand what the Father was communicating in the gospel according to John 3:16, NKJV: *"For God so loved the world that He gave His only begotten Son, that whosoever believes in Him should not perish but have everlasting life."*

I thought and reflected, "How much love does it take for one to give their child to someone else to raise without being able to love and provide for that child as a mother?" I clearly understood the depth of deception and how it can separate people based on what is perceived versus what is true. I took the time to reflect on the truth of what God had revealed. I called my mother and told her I wanted to speak with her. As we sat down to talk, I said, "I forgive you," and asked for forgiveness as well. I confessed to her that I had accepted some lies and deception from the enemy as truth. True breakthrough was evident in my heart. I knew that it did not matter what other versions of the story were still circulating about; I embraced *God's Truth* in the matter. It was finished. My moment of breakthrough was so much more than I could have ever imagined. I realized I had elevated above an earthly awareness and rose to a Kingdom clarity of heart and mindset in the heavenlies. I was no longer compelled to blame myself or anyone else.

I learned so many things in that week. I had been allowing programs and religious structure to dictate my relationship with the Father, and I want to expound upon that concept. I had not realized just how much time was being given to announcements, offerings, and other things which had no direct bearing on my personal relationship with God. At the same time, I noticed how little time was spent truly worshiping the Lord and encountering His presence for real transformation and breakthrough.

The week I spent in His presence touched a place inside me that I didn't know existed: Jesus was in me... His Kingdom was in me. It took me a while to spiritually unpack what the Lord had done in my spirit over the course of that week. But I am grateful for the FatherHeart Ministries and how their passionate pursuit of God's heart impacted my life so tremendously.

The more I received from the Lord, the more He began to empty everything in my life: my family and even the perception I had of them toward ministry. My marriage and family relationships began to transform. This was my introduction to the Kingdom of God. Equally as important, I was able to renounce and break agreement with the spirit of religion. Honestly, it took me a while to fully grasp what I had experienced during that week. Yet, I knew things were going to be different for me moving forward.

In those moments of worship, I understood my perspective wasn't the Lord's perspective. Therefore, it was not true. Ultimately, I understood the way I had thought and had believed all my life was not of God, nor was it His heart toward me. The Word of the Lord had broken through and pierced my spirit. I had received my heavenly Father's heart! I could see how important it was to renew my mind and walk in forgiveness. When you receive the Father's heart, you will receive a greater level of knowledge of how your flesh has been deceived and its impact on your thoughts and belief system.

The real breakthrough comes when you embrace truth about yourself, especially as it pertains to the way you think and process truth. If you don't have a clear perception of yourself, it will be impossible to have a clear perception of others. In other words, if you see your life through a clouded lens where you continually feel like someone did something to you, this is a victim's lens. I'm not suggesting adverse things won't happen, it's just that if you continue to hold on to the past, things will never change completely in your life.

Whatever it is that may be clouding you from seeing things through the eyes of Christ, please know that it's blocking your capacity to receive God's love and the blessings of sonship. Let… it… go. Turn off all your electronic devices. Dedicate intentional, quality time (not just a few random moments) with God as your only focus. It will change the trajectory of your life. Tap into His presence in worship both in your prayer closet and in corporate worship opportunities to pursue Holy Spirit's presence like never before. I promise your life will never be the same.

If you are a leader in the Body of Christ, once you've received the Father's heart and your personal revelatory breakthrough, I encourage you to seek Him on behalf of your congregation and leadership teams. Discover how you can partner with the Holy Spirit to create an atmosphere for breakthroughs and divine encounters for your ministry to experience His presence and glory on a regular basis. There is one thing that I hope will catapult you into seeking God on this encounter level: don't be selfish in your perspective as I had been. All the beliefs and understanding surrounding my family were centered around me and my pain. I made it about me, so this gave the enemy access to block the blessings from flowing into my life. Now I can say with all confidence, I know who I really am in the eyes of Christ. I also live out my life daily with the mind of Christ. Therefore, I can authentically embrace my God-given purpose, authority, and blessings as His beloved son.

The breakthrough experience brought me into a more intimate place with the Father as His son. This time of intimacy was so loving, reassuring, and safe. The Lord of the breakthrough began to speak to me directly, and He brought a treasure trove of clarity which enabled me to embrace His loving and compassionate heart. Intimacy removes all the barriers that inhibit us from receiving from the Lord. These encounters also allowed me to trust God more deeply. My Father had invited me into transformational experiences in the realm of the Spirit. It was so powerful to catch the revelation that I am truly seated in heavenly places with Him.

Previously, when I'd thought about breakthrough, I always thought how it would empower me to overcome the enemy. However, the encounter with the Father's heart should not only empower us, but also teach us to focus on God's prophetic insight and truths, not ours. The more we tap into His presence, the more we will start to realize that breakthrough encounters are not just for the purpose of intimacy. It's so profound when you realize that God really wants to impart His wisdom so we can better demonstrate His Kingdom on the earth and help others throughout the nations to experience His unconditional love.

Chapter Eight

Sonship

I've gained some powerful insights concerning sonship in both the natural and spiritual realms. Both have enriched my life tremendously. Through this book it is my hope that everyone will take the time to look back through their life story through a spiritual lens. The acceptance of a natural father is the first part of deciphering the code of sonship. This scripture makes it very clear that we should honor our parents. According to Ephesians 6:1-4 (NKJV): *"Children, obey your parents in the Lord, for this is right. Honor your father and mother, which is the first commandment with promise: that it may be well with you and you may live long on the earth. And you, fathers do not provoke your children to wrath, but bring them up in the training and admonition of the Lord."*

I started with the goal of providing a few highlights from my personal path. However, as I journeyed through more chapters, I found this had turned into a more comprehensive approach to personal discoveries. This helped me to grasp a more detailed understanding of the father-son relationship. That's what I will share in this chapter regarding the things I once considered painful. By looking at this through the Holy Spirit's perspective, it brought me to a place of more spiritual awareness which facilitated discovering my true identity. It's interesting when I refer to a "place," as it's not a physical or emotional place; it's actually a position I received in Christ as a son of God.

This is the bedrock of everything moving forward in our personal relationship with the Holy Spirit. The passage above from Ephesians makes a reference to the obedience and honor we should extend toward our parents. In the natural, it's normal to look at behaviors and default to negative thoughts regarding our experiences. Yet, God gave these commandments to honor and obey. He never placed conditions on our parents to fulfil criteria to be worthy of honor. We should simply honor them regardless of circumstances or negative behaviors. Blessings will automatically flow because of obedience to His Word.

Once my heart was aligned and postured as an authentic son of God, I started to realize it wasn't about how my father lived or even what he believed. It really came down to my desire to relinquish *my* will. In other words, I had to die to myself to walk fully submitted in obedience to God's Word. This became my baseline for understanding how honor truly works. The Lord places parents in the position to receive honor from children. If we are to honor our imperfect natural parents, how much easier it should be to honor our heavenly Father who is perfect? As I reflect back, I can remember many times when I didn't really honor either my parents or my grandparents. Thankfully, I've gained a much deeper understanding of obedience over the years which has helped me to understand the importance of honor.

The church gatherings I'd witnessed always seemed to judge how others acted. Culturally speaking, I didn't understand that many church environments were behaviorally focused. With that type of focus on actions and behaviors, it only contributed to the lack of understanding I had regarding my identity. Accepting my true identity in Christ created more freedom because of my position relationally with the Father. My perspective on what it meant to be a disciple of Christ was fractured at best. I had been influenced by my home life and family structure, the same things universally experienced in all humanity. Once I received the Truth that I am a son of God, I knew my life experience in the family was severely flawed. Most importantly, I thought the revelation of "born in sin and shaped in iniquity" had impacted my entire life. It even influenced how I received the knowledge of Christ.

The great news is that *"all things work together"* for our good. The more I allowed the Holy Spirit to help me gain clarity in my life, the more I realized I had not completely stepped into my position as a son of God. The role that my family and church had played in shaping my identity in Christ was huge. Now it makes total sense.

A term which was very familiar to me growing up in the church was: "a sinner saved by grace." However, the focus on sonship was rarely taught. It was never a priority in the biblical teachings. It wasn't until later in life in my personal relationship with Christ that I began to receive Him as more than a Savior. There were so many things I needed the Lord to rewrite in my life concerning family for me to receive His Truth. I needed to understand clearly how to delineate between the truths manufactured by my emotions versus what Holy Spirit said were *His* Truth. The only way I knew to accomplish such a monumental task was to begin with the raw facts.

To streamline my process, I started with my heart. All the feelings and thoughts I had swirling around in my head had to be exposed and laid down. Those thoughts had to be brought into captivity so that only The Truth could prevail. In the position of authority as a son of God, I was able to cast down vain imaginations. Instead of thinking about my desired outcome, my prayers changed dramatically to simply ask my Father to give me prophetic insight and His wisdom.

The moment I was given to my grandparents was the moment the physical connection with my immediate family was broken. This created a ripple effect of emotional and spiritual disconnect as well.

So, it is with tender loving care that I must share the next part in this journey. It's an extremely sensitive area which I don't want to be misconstrued, but I had an emotional and spiritual break when I was separated from my biological family. The separation caused me to have an emptiness in my heart that only God's Truth could fill. I had no one to help me understand what those feelings and emotions were or how to process them from God's heavenly viewpoint. There was a deeply rooted void in my soul. My mind, will, and emotions were all influenced by this physical disconnection from my parents. Unfortunately, because there is so much brokenness and dysfunction in countless families across the world, there are many others who have had or will experience similar situations and feelings in their lives. However, there is hope and freedom by surrendering to the process. The Holy Spirit can and will bring about true healing and deliverance in your life. It's key to first acknowledge the Truth. That's when the process of embracing your true identity as a son of God can begin.

We've all entered this world in different ways, some planned, and some unplanned. Regardless of your route into this world, God wants you to know that it's okay to acknowledge His Truth. It is what prevails and overtakes those negative thoughts and emotions in the process. In other words, simply embrace this time as Holy Spirit ministers to you. Allow this encounter with the Lord to saturate every area of your heart as a beautiful "moment of release." Acknowledge all the emotions surrounding your entry into this world and any associated trauma or pain. Then allow the Holy Spirit to comfort you as Jesus ministers healing to your heart.

As with my own testimony, this might be the one time in your life to openly accept the truth about your life experiences so that your true identity as a son can arise. The enemy manipulated my story to prevent me from walking in wholeness. He caused me to live in somewhat of a spiritual coma. It seemed as though I was only able to breathe laboriously between facts and Truth. I overcame the pain and all the drama thanks to my relationship with my Father. Now, I truly see myself the way my Father sees me, and so can you.

As I began to embrace sonship, my spirit-man was revived, and I received more revelation surrounding my family as a son of God. I realized God has given men the grace to speak life over their wives and children. He designed men to transform family legacies for generations to come. So, when a man doesn't step up to fulfill that responsibility, the family dynamic will be out of order. Father God knew the importance of affirmation over a son, which is why He made it crystal clear during His beloved son Jesus's baptism. He revealed who Jesus was and affirmed His identity. God went even further to edify His Son's identity by giving affirmation when John baptized Jesus according to Matthew 3:16-17 (NKJV): [16]*"When He had been baptized, Jesus came up immediately from the water;*

and behold, the heavens were opened to Him, and He saw the Spirit of God descending like a dove and alighting upon Him. ^{17}And suddenly a voice came from heaven, saying, 'This is My beloved Son, in whom I am well pleased.' " The affirmation of children by both parents means everything, but especially when it comes from their father.

Interestingly enough, I never had my father or grandfather (nor any men from the church where I grew up) speak words of "life" and confirmation over me as a child. So, it is like the saying goes, "You don't know what you don't know." When the affirmation and impartation of identity experience is missing from a child's early years of life, it can prohibit the son or daughter from recognizing who they really are. I questioned everything about myself until I embraced my position as a son of God. It's unfortunate that we all have walked through this misidentification where our adversary takes full advantage through deception. As I surrendered to this process of discovering Truth, I started to realize that the enemy had taken every opportunity to distract me with pain and feelings of not being accepted or affirmed by my father.

The next reality had a tremendous bearing on my inability to see God as Father when I was growing up. I had a very close relationship with my father, or so I thought. After further examination it began to become obvious that it was a friendship not a father-son relationship. I remember a time when I was maybe sixteen or so when my father and I were at the community park. It was during a time when CB radios were very popular. My father had one, and his CB radio "handle" was Charleston Blue. I thought the CB handle was really fun and cool, but never recognized that it lacked the honor which the Bible speaks about. So, I decided to have a conversation with my dad about referring to him as something other than "Dad." In my mind, *Dad* just didn't really fit. I knew he was my biological father, but our bond seemed more like a great friendship. I wanted a name to reflect how I viewed our connection. So, I came up with the name, Charles. It was a variation of his CB handle. He seemed to like it, so I referred to him as Charles for the remainder of his life.

We've all experienced things both good and bad in our lives. These experiences create perceptions and ultimately belief systems about ourselves and the world around us. The main issue with my perception was that it originated from things I thought and felt due to my lack of knowledge surrounding sonship. Instead of relying on what the Holy Spirit of Truth would later reveal through this process, I relied on the pain and feelings from my lack of identity. My perceptions were not met with Truth. Instead, over time, they became *my* truth, not God's Truth.

The fact that my father and I were not in the same physical home had a tremendous influence on the way I viewed my dad. Like most of us with similar familial experiences, I just didn't understand. I needed a natural father to step in with the Truth of the Word of God and confront how I felt and how I thought. I did not recognize it then, but I was using his absence (along with the emotional absence of my grandfather) to form my own definition of sonship. As a result, my thoughts and feelings were real. This was part of the reason it became critical for me to revisit my story. It was essential to look back over my family experiences with a Holy Spirit viewpoint, and not with my broken heart. It was only then that I could allow the Holy Spirit to untangle all the ungodly misperceptions I had formed in my mind. It became so much easier at that point to see through the eyes of Christ.

When facts become our teacher instead of Truth, they can easily cause us to form misconceived thoughts, thus prompting us to embrace a false identity. Then what we experience in life can cause us to be shaken. The Truth should come from scripture and should cause us to be stable in all our ways. The connection between father and son is what sets the stage for a solid understanding of our heavenly Father. Anytime there are breaks of any kind in our families, especially between a father and son, it can easily be mentally processed as pain. Our spiritual identity comes from our heavenly Father. When I arrived at a place in my heart by faith where I could receive more than the forgiveness of my sins from Christ on the cross, then I received the revelation of sonship.

The twenty plus years I have spent in ministry has produced deep wells of wisdom of His Truth in my spirit. As a result, God has placed the mantle of an apostolic father over me. He has blessed my wife and me with many amazing sons and daughters to walk with. We encourage each other and help each other to unlock the mysteries of "sonship" to affirm our identities in Christ. The Father desires to have sons and daughters who mature so they can view life from the vantage point of a son. His divine multiplication plan is for us to produce other sons and daughters, to be fruitful in all Kingdom matters. I'm so thankful for the grace I've been given to father the next generation and impact families for God's glory. Now when I look back to what I perceived as hard places, I understand it was just an opportunity to grow.

I know it was the grace of God that kept me while I was living life out of alignment and position as His son. It is the position of sonship that is one of the greatest benefits of the redemptive process of Jesus. According to Romans 8:12-17 (NKJV): *"Therefore, brethren, we are debtors-not to the flesh, to live according to the flesh. For if you live according to the flesh you will die; but if by the Spirit you put to death the deeds of the body, you will live. For as many as are led by the Spirit of God, these are sons of God. For you did not receive the spirit of bondage again to fear, but you received the Spirit of adoption by whom we cry out, 'Abba, Father.' The Spirit Himself bears witness with our spirit, and confirms we are the children of God, and if children, then heirs of God and joint heirs with Christ, if indeed we suffer with Him, that we may also be glorified together."*

This scripture makes it very clear that our relationship with God is spiritual; it's not based on our flesh or will. The Holy Spirit serves as confirmation that we are indeed the sons of God. To take it a step further, when Jesus died on the cross and shed His blood, His sacrifice not only extended forgiveness for our sins, it also enabled us to receive the Spirit of Adoption. Our sonship status and position give us the right to live freely in Christ. I encourage you to continue to speak this Truth throughout your journey to reaffirm your position in Christ: "I am a son/daughter of God. My heavenly Father has accepted me as His son/daughter with all the rights and privileges in the family of God."

Romans 8:28 NKJV - *And we know that all things work together for good to those who love God, to those who are the called according to His purpose.*

Chapter 9

Redeeming Love

It is of a certainty that I can say this: there is residue from the dysfunction in our families, relationships, and past friendships. It shows up in our lives and continues a cycle of restlessness. These issues were hiding in plain sight in my life, and I started to realize the need to be set free from them completely. As I became a young adult, I really didn't understand the magnitude of the residual pain from my childhood. This further exacerbated the impact because I didn't acknowledge that my issues needed to be dealt with. One of the ways I could have dealt with those areas would have been to simply talk it out with my family. I started to discover that communication was not possible because my point of view was skewed by my past life experiences. It had become my belief system that if it was important, the appropriate response was to keep it a secret. To communicate my feelings and thoughts to someone significant in my life, like my grandmother, would have only added to the pain I was already experiencing.

When I was a young adult, I was unaware how unresolved emotional issues can create opportunities for the enemy to plant seeds of doubt, which then lead to unbelief. The moment we experience trauma or abuse of any kind, the enemy takes advantage of us in those areas. He then uses those moments to infiltrate our thoughts and plant seeds of doubt, low self-esteem, rejection, and anything else that's negative surrounding our true identity as a son. These types of thoughts can easily lead a person to see themselves through their experiences rather than who they are.

The most profound discovery I unlocked as I looked back at my story through the viewpoint of Holy Spirit, is that I didn't know the thoughts and mindset I had at the time were from the enemy in the first place. I really believed they were my own thoughts. I believed it was all true because I was given away, and no one took the time to explain "why." My life boiled down to that one decision... a decision I had no control over. This created a huge opening in my heart where the enemy fed me more lies, and it was upon these lies that my belief system ultimately was built.

Most of my young adulthood was lived out as a "fixer." I thought my problems were mine alone to fix. The scriptures make it very plain in NKJV Hosea 4:6(a): *"My people are destroyed for lack of knowledge."* I was clueless about this spiritual dynamic. The events of my life were like puzzle pieces which needed connections in truth (both natural and spiritual) to even begin to understand God's desire of who He had created me to become. I felt like I had a gaping hole in my heart. So instead of going to the Lord in prayer, I tried to fix it *my* way. My drug of choice became the alluring presence of women. I thought if I could just get married and start my own family, things would be fine. The moment I started developing serious feelings for someone, I got married. I didn't do counseling or speak to anyone like a pastor. I simply ran off, and seven months later, I welcomed a baby boy into the world.

The thing about taking matters into your own hands is you can't see it at the time, but it always costs you more. I couldn't see the house I'd built was on the sand of my emotions and not on the stability of scripture. According to Matthew 7: 24-27 (NKJV): [24] *"Therefore whoever hears these sayings of Mine, and does them, I will liken him to a wise man who built his house on the rock:* [25] *and the rain descended, the floods came, and the winds blew and beat on that house; and it did not fall, for it was founded on the rock.*[26] *"But everyone who hears these sayings of Mine, and does not do them, will be like a foolish man who built his house on the sand:* [27] *and the rain descended, the floods came, and the winds blew and beat on that house; and it fell. And great was its fall."*

    The marriage I abruptly jumped into was a failed attempt at resolving my heart and family and relationship issues. When you don't have the knowledge, and you don't seek counsel, it's easy to think what you're doing is the right thing. I spent less than five years in a union before it came crashing to the ground just like the latter part of the scripture mentions. The hardest thing for me at the time wasn't just the stain of divorce, it was knowing my unresolved issues would cause my son similar pain.

    While I recognized I didn't have anything to do with being born into this world or family dynamic, it was all too real that this chapter of my life was totally *my* decision. This was the first time in my life when I clearly saw how unresolved issues in family must be addressed. Even as an adult, I still felt like I had reasonable questions surrounding my childhood. I was greatly impacted as a result, and now my flawed decisions were impacting my first-born son.

    Next, when my son's mother decided to move out of state, I was devastated. Why would she move out of state? It must be me again, the "unworthy" father. Needless to say, this impacted my connection with my son while he was young. It not only escalated the feelings of unworthiness to have a family, it negatively influenced our father-son relationship. I was at a place emotionally where the enemy made it easy for me to believe the lie that since I was divorced, I was not good enough to have a family. This became yet another false "truth" in my beliefs. However, I now understand that lack of knowledge keeps us in the dark. So, to embrace the Truth of the Word of God, our thoughts and feelings need to be exposed to the light of His Word. His light is what dispels darkness. This is the only way to redemption, reconciliation, and restoration in important relationships in our lives.

Now let's delve deeper into how my son's mother leaving the state impacted me. My heart was so fractured that I didn't even think about the possibility of partial custody; I just became complicit to her decision. This only fortified the false beliefs and plots of the enemy to keep me in darkness and despair. Specifically, he drilled it in that because my birth family rejected me, I would never be worthy enough to have my own family. I just didn't realize at the time that they were all lies...

The enemy always wanted me to focus on what was in front of me from a victim's perspective, but he always has a bigger agenda than what we can see. He wasn't just trying to keep me in an emotional whirlwind. That was just the "set up." He blinded me to see what was *good* in my life. Ultimately, his goal was to steal my identity as a son of God, kill my peace, and destroy my father-son relationship with my firstborn.

Interestingly, my relationship with God also suffered during that time in my adult life. My self-esteem began to evaporate like water hitting a hot pavement. I was imprisoned by my emotions, and every time I came before the parole board of my mind, I was denied freedom. The Bible speaks of the accuser of the brethren according to Revelation 12:10 (b) (NKJV): *"For the accuser of our brethren, who accused them before our God day and night, has been cast down."* I believed that I had been given away because my family didn't really want me, so why would anyone else want me? The more I thought about my life and my decisions, the more shame and guilt tried to squeeze the life out of me.

So, the beliefs surrounding my identity then became strongholds, and everything the enemy had said to me my entire life became more ingrained in me. I didn't belong anywhere. I had failed at every attempt at being a part of a family. The things that had taken place in my life seemed to line up with the lies the enemy had whispered in my ear. It's what made it so believable. I mentioned in a previous chapter about how I thought things were happening *to* me. It took me time to understand things were really happening *for* me. I just needed to make a godly connection through Holy Spirit's guidance. Yet, I still had not come out of the woods. I was a mess. It started getting harder to get up and go through the day. This part of my story I've only shared at surface level. I didn't want anyone to know just how close to the edge I really was.

One of the main things the enemy whispered in my ear was to stay silent. I was convinced that to keep those feelings inside was the best action, and following the example of my family is what God, Himself, expected of me. They were lies, and I was embracing them as truth. Please understand this: the enemy wants you to separate yourself from people and to self-medicate. He doesn't care what you do to bring yourself emotional relief; he just doesn't want you talking to anyone. The goal of the enemy is to kill, steal, and destroy. I started to think the whole world was against me and things would never get better. Once you start to think like that, the enemy has an opening and can begin the process of stealing your identity in Christ.

The other huge lie from the enemy is the Lord is paying you back for past (or present) sins. It's all lies according to John 3:17: *"For God did not send His Son into the world to condemn the world, but that the world through Him might be saved."* The enemy comes into places in our lives where our belief system doesn't line up with the truth from the Word of God. When we don't know the truth or don't apply the truth in our lives, it gives the enemy a "foothold" to attack us with deception to further separate us from Jesus, **the** Truth. He uses emotional trauma to twist truth so he can inject us with poisonous lies.

I am so grateful that our Father turned around all those things that the enemy meant for harm. According to Romans 8:28-29 (NKJV): *"And we know that all things work together for the good to those who love God, to those who are the called according to His purpose. For whom He foreknew, He also predestined to be conformed to the image of His Son, that He might be the first born among many brethren."*

One of the things I was able to embrace about this scripture is we're predestined to be conformed to the image of the Son of God. God didn't cause the tough things to happen in life, but because of the enemy's tactics to steal, kill, and destroy, our Father makes it work together for our good. The power of this scripture started happening for me when I started to renew my mind. God is faithful and will do the same for you.

When I was going through those tough emotions, I felt shame, guilt, and a host of other things which didn't have anything to do with the love of God. It helped me to understand how important it is to be in the center of His will. The real change came for me when I met a lady at a vending machine in the hallway at my place of employment. She told me she was having a gathering of friends at her house for the upcoming holiday, and she wanted to know if I would be interested to drop by. I have to be honest; I was afraid to say "yes," but was equally daunted to say "no." I was still fighting to gain control of my mind and my emotions. She gave me her number, and I finally decided to call and accept the invitation. I had no idea this short exchange at a vending machine would be the start of a journey which would change my entire life. When I think back to that moment, I don't even remember what I purchased from the machine. It really doesn't matter. The fact is I was still weak, but the Lord had mercy on me and strengthened me enough to make a phone call.

We ended up getting to know each other and we realized how different we were in background and life experiences. However, as it turned out, our hearts desired the same thing. We both simply wanted to be loved the way God intended for us. We were not aware at the time how much we both needed heart and mindset transformation, but God did.

Then I did something I had never done before. I began to share. I realized my history was too important to keep it locked away in my heart. Breaking the silence brought me freedom. I began to realize how much I had been restricting myself by not talking.

My transformation began in a hallway at a vending machine. The change for you may come through your career, a new business, or a hobby, etc. It may be the conversation you've longed to have. It may come in the way the Lord touches your heart after the loss of a family member. I can't tell you the way the Lord will move in your life, but I can assure you He wants to move in you and through you. He doesn't want you to linger in the past of what could have been. Instead, I promise you'll benefit with greater wisdom and insight regarding truth by being thankful for what was (and has been) revealed surrounding your life experiences.

I spent too much time carrying the pain of believing I wasn't loved. I was convinced my parents gave me away because I wasn't worthy of their affection or attention. I had multiple visits to a professional counselor. I surrendered to the process of healing my broken heart. I invested time in prayer. Other times I just talked about how I felt with people who could help me and who loved me through those times. I learned how to not judge others. I no longer hold grudges and can now genuinely and sincerely pray for people that have mistreated me. I learned how to lean into my relationship with my heavenly Father and live a holistic, balanced lifestyle. This made the difference in me. It is indeed a process. Yet now I can sincerely say I love myself and forgive myself for believing the false perceptions of my past.

Our Father has a plan for all our lives. He also has a way of protecting us even when we don't know we need to be protected. Now, I see the things I experienced in life surrounding hurt, disappointment, discouragement, shame, and guilt with a sense of freedom, and in some cases, humor. I now realize the meaning of the scripture that reveals that even when we don't know what to ask Him for, the Holy Spirit knows all. I recognized I had been asking Him to fix me and deliver me from something that wasn't even truth.

He's omniscient. He knew all my struggles. But this was my pre-destined pathway for deliverance. All along I was expecting Him to "fix" what went wrong in my life when He didn't cause those things to happen in the first place. I didn't need it to be fixed; I needed to understand it.

I faced a decision at that vending machine. How could I pick up the phone when I was still struggling with my emotions? I knew I wasn't about to trust my feelings. I needed God's help. I also needed someone with a godly perspective in my life. I was determined to not let the things from my past stop me. I also decided to go back to church. I desperately needed my Father and wanted Him to know I now understood the truth about my past. I knew I couldn't trust my heart or emotions... Not this time.

I remember being in church on a Sunday morning, knowing the Lord had created the path for me to find her, my wife-to-be. I will never forget when the pastor finished his message and asked people to come to the front for prayer. I was compelled to get out of my seat. I was drawn to the altar and knew it was the Holy Spirit.

I fell on my knees and asked for forgiveness. I was tired of trying to do it my way and of carrying all the emotional weight of my past. I had reached a place where I wanted to give it all over to Jesus. He never made me feel bad for trying to fix my life without asking for His help. He just poured out His unconditional love. The difference was I was finally ready to receive it. The Father met me at the altar, and I felt His overwhelming love pouring over me like the relief of rain on a hot summer day. When I looked up, I noticed my girl was right beside me on her knees crying out to the Lord. I can't put words to what I experienced that day. It was like He took all my thoughts and feelings from years of emotional pain and rejection and allowed my tears to wash the impact away. I knew in that moment I had fully surrendered to His love.

The same lady I met in a hallway at a vending machine has been my wife for over thirty years now. I'm still thankful. Twenty-five plus of those years we have spent in ministry serving alongside each other discipling and training leaders to lead well. We've seen both the worst of times and the best of times. Thankfully, we have done it together.

We both acknowledge that the only way we were able to do it was through the redeeming blood of Jesus Christ. I had to reach a place in my mind to allow the Holy Spirit to heal those areas in my heart and empower me to cast down those vain imaginations to no longer feel the need to try to "carry the burdens" myself. I've only mentioned a few of the things I went through, but I know that if it were not for the blood of Jesus, I wouldn't be writing this book.

Chapter 10

I can see clearly now the pain is gone

For most of my life, I questioned whether I was worthy to be loved. It started when my grandparents assumed parental responsibilities; I thought something was wrong with me if my parents didn't want to raise me. In my mind, it was one thing for my grandparents to have custody. Yet, because I never received answers, it only added to my already preconceived notion that perhaps I was not worthy of love. I remember the few times that I attended family reunions (although I rarely attended), I never felt like I belonged. I remember my grandmother introducing me to other family members saying, "This is Johnnie's child." No one ever named both my parents when introducing me; it was always only my father. This was so confusing and even hurtful because my grandmother unfailingly treated me like I was her child at home. But at these gatherings, she always made a point to share that I was *Johnnie's* son.

I look back at my time spent in church as a child. There was no information shared or instruction imparted to teach me about inner healing or matters of the heart. It's interesting now to reflect on this lack of knowledge. I can see clearly now that it was Father God Himself who imparted me with wisdom and ignited passion on the importance of healing those areas in my heart so I could embrace my identity in Christ. It was a matter of simply accepting the *agape* love of our Father to overcome the emotional trauma that I felt as a child. Once I understood the truth, I was able to move forward to renew my mind.

The renewal of the mind is of the utmost importance in reaching a place of wholeness and freedom in life. When you really "renew your mind," you take on the mind of Christ. That's where the true victory is. Then you can start coming into agreement with the fullness of your identity. When there is no more ambiguity regarding your identity, you can confidently declare, "I am who God says I am." I implore you to allow the Holy Spirit to heal those areas in your heart so that the emotional and mental baggage of your past no longer plagues your mind. Jesus already gave His life by shedding His blood so that we all can be healed and experience freedom throughout our lives in the Kingdom.

Once I began to realize the healing and deliverance in my life, my heavenly Father revealed even more for me. It is never a "one and done" experience. For me, this was only a very intensive start to the journey of healing and freedom. One of the most important things that I did after the ministry of inner healing and deliverance was to call my mother. I was well into adulthood by now, so I took the approach of responsibility and accountability when I told her I wanted to talk. I didn't go into detail about the "what" or "why," but I believe she knew.

When I was a young child, she would never talk to me about what had transpired. It frustrated me for a long time until I allowed the Holy Spirit to take me further into the healing of my heart. I want to share a wisdom key with you right here. I propose this piece is just as significant in concept of heart healing and identity. It was essential for me to release all past thoughts and feelings of judgment and condemnation and meet my mother where she was emotionally, mentally, and spiritually. Too often in the past, I had approached these types of conversations with fear or a lack of openness to allow the Holy Spirit to lead me into what to say. It never works if you bring your own preconceived notions to the table of conversation. It's why I wholeheartedly believe the healing of our hearts must occur before we approach a loved one with difficult conversations.

When I finally spoke to her, I simply told my mother that it didn't matter what really happened. Everybody makes mistakes. Then it became so much easier to live from the place of forgiveness and the freedom which Jesus extends to us all. I accepted whatever she said as her best description and responses of our journey as mother and son. After that, I never looked back or yearned for better or clearer answers. I actually don't even have further questions. I was able to simply let the previous burden to ask deeper questions go. The thing that made it manageable was to acknowledge that we cannot change the past no matter how good it was or how traumatic it was; we only need to come to terms with it. My mother and I both needed closure to heal our wounds from the pain that stemmed from decades of silence.

Another thing I began to consider that I never saw before, was the impact of the pain my mother may have felt regarding giving me to my grandparents. What did it mean to the heart of a mother who never held me in her arms as a baby or nurtured me through significant milestones in life? Then I pondered what had been going on in the heart of my grandmother, knowing she was raising another woman's child? My heart was more open to receive the Father's selfless compassion and insight now that my heart was healed. I began to see things through the lens of a loving Father, not my own selfishness.

Soon afterwards, I was finally able to accept the fact I was not responsible for how I entered this world. The moment that switch came on, it aided me to accept and appreciate the life and freedom I enjoy today. Even though we cannot change the past, thankfully, the redeeming love of Jesus has the power to break every chain in our lives. We must let Him do the work to help us let go.

The greatest miracle for me was when my heavenly Father asked me to write this book. I never realized how this would bring even more healing and breakthrough in my life. I am so thankful now that I took Him up on the invitation. It has given me an opportunity to share matters of my heart. This is even more essential because through this book and the testimony of my journey, this will reach additional generations who have gone through similar experiences.

I pray this will encourage you to take another look at your own story, to look for those painful moments from your past, because you may discover your "facts" may not be His *truth*. I had peace the moment I understood life isn't about assigning blame to anyone or trying to get answers to questions which won't change the outcome of the past. It's about exposing and then letting go of things which have had an emotional stranglehold. It really does make forgiveness easy. It also becomes easier to recognize the opportunity to flip the script from "Lord, why me?" to "Father, forgive them for they know not what they've done." Also ask yourself how *your* testimony might help someone else receive breakthrough in this area.

I started to hear the voice of my Father saying, "I'm right here with you." I also realized that I couldn't see

Him as my loving Father during the painful times when I believed I was not worthy of family ties. It almost took my breath away. But reflecting now, I know that He was the *closest* to me in those times, comforting me through my tears. I love my family. I understand they're not perfect, but neither am I. God still loves us all. I've learned so much over the years through what I've gone through. It has humbled me; I just strive to reveal humanity to others in a way I hope makes Christ seen. Now that I've surrendered to the process of the "heart work" to be healed, I see the main thing Father God wanted me to know all along is that I am His beloved son.

When we make life about what our experiences are instead of what our victories should be, we minimize our footprint on the earth. I see that now. If we're constantly confessing how we are beat down by life, even if this is just to ourselves, we don't show Christ in the best light. I can almost hear you say, "But you don't know or understand what I've been through." That is very true. I don't know what happened to you. Yet, I can promise you this: none of us have gone through what Jesus went through willingly for us.

The process of being developed in His image is not something which we raise our hand to sign up for. The process of getting to the knowledge and insight from the Holy Spirit is never easy; it takes diligence and reaffirmation to change thought processes to align with the truth of God's Word. However, the work invested will be worth it. Pride is crushed and uncertainty is vanquished when mindsets align with the Truth. God knows the deepest crevices of our hearts, so the process leading up to sharing our stories with others is essential to ensure He gets all the glory for the breakthrough.

If your focus is only on the pain when you share your story, revisit it again through prayer, then surrender to the journey of healing your heart. Boldly proclaim victory and how you overcame it! Otherwise, you are making the enemy look larger than Jesus. Sharing past pain which also aligns with the biblical steps taken to reach victory, highlights Jesus. He is the only way to salvation, healing, and victory. If the focus is only on the pain, and that's all that gets communicated, this gives more attention to the enemy. Keep mindful that all the glory and honor belongs to our Father God.

The enemy always leverages the brokenness in our hearts to gain access to our minds to continually taunt and manipulate us. I had many encounters with the Father long before I sat down to write this book. The Father was not only transforming my heart, He was restoring my spiritual vision to see His Truth so that I could begin to see myself and others the way He does. Don't allow past trauma to create a false identity. Search the scriptures and claim who you are in Christ; claim your position as a son of the most high God.

When I spoke in a previous chapter about pain and how it didn't belong to me, note that I am not saying that we should pretend the pain is not real. I want to make it crystal clear that the wounds of abandonment, rejection, and not belonging will cause legitimate emotional hurt in our soul (mind, will, and emotions). However, what your Father wants you to know, is that you never were meant to "own" the pain and wrap your identity around it. Yes... It occurred... Period. Yet thankfully your story doesn't end there. It is a fresh beginning to receive the love of the Father by allowing Him to heal broken areas in your heart. Once you surrender to the process, your mind will shift to the truth so your spiritual sight will no longer be skewed. Your story becomes the testimony of Jesus Christ and how you overcame the enemy by His blood. Your mindset will shift from, "What happened to me, belongs to me," to *"Casting all our cares upon Him..."* You will begin to speak life instead of brokenness, and many of you will write books or speak publicly on your overcomer's story. The optics of your spiritual sight will be restored to Truth so others will hear the Word of God, receive the Truth about who God says they are, and surrender to their own process of healing and deliverance.

I had places in my life where people and things caused me pain, but I needed to be accountable for my part. I wasn't responsible or accountable as a child born into this world. This is such an important statement; it's a connection to the maturation process. The more I matured in my relationship with God, the more I understood the pain of my past was not my identity. It never was, nor will it ever be. It was simply a direct result of what parents/grandparents didn't teach me. It may sound like I'm still blaming them, but once my heart was healed, God restored my spiritual sight to His original design and lens of truth. The Holy Spirit enlightened me to see (and know) *the* Truth. That's true freedom. It wasn't that my parents didn't love me; they lacked the knowledge in Christ to take authority over the enemy's tactics.

I discovered soon afterward that the things I thought I understood in the natural were not completely true. Subsequently, the things in the spiritual realm where I didn't have a clue made everything harder for me to see or comprehend. As people have said, "You don't know what you don't know."

I have spent so much time over the years as a pastor and apostolic leader helping people understand how parents and others who caused them pain were also attacked and tormented by the enemy. Unfortunately, he has taken advantage of all of us in one way or another. Yet, we must note that it does not remove our accountability. It does, however, make it much easier to forgive and release the emotional burden.

Psalm 51: 10-12 (ESV): "¹⁰Create in me a clean heart, O God, and renew a right spirit within me. ¹¹Cast me not away from your presence and take not your Holy Spirit from me. ¹²Restore to me the joy of your salvation and uphold me with a willing spirit."

It took this journey with Holy Spirit to open my eyes of understanding. This was the doorway of Jesus Christ to the Truth. Now I am free indeed. I have taken responsibility in my first son's life and for the pain I caused him. I've forgiven my family and have asked for their forgiveness as well. I've also forgiven myself for believing falsely for so many years of my life. This is true freedom and deliverance. It's an awesome opportunity now to share the love of God, His revealed knowledge, and to impart godly wisdom to all my children to break the cycle in our lineage by the power of Holy Spirit. I overcame every lie and broke every false agreement with the enemy to reach this place of victory. I can see clearly now that I view myself, my family, and ministry through the eyes of my Father. You can too!

Chapter 11

All things work together

I've spent a tremendous amount of time thinking and praying about how to share my story, aiming to maintain honor and grace for my parents and grandparents throughout the narrative. My view of family, and my place within it, was hewn by the dysfunctional experiences I endured in two vastly different homes. My father's house embodied chaos and disruption. That was the norm, and it prevented the family from ever coming together as a cohesive unit. As a child, I never quite understood why I was given to my grandparents. The secrecy surrounding this decision often made me wonder if there were other elements of the truth they were withholding from me. Over time, I reached a point where I stopped wondering altogether. However, it was a long and arduous process to get there.

Growing up in my grandparents' home presented a completely different atmosphere. My grandmother's home exuded quiet and peace, which was a stark contrast to the turmoil experienced at my father's house. It almost seems ironic to describe it this way, knowing my grandfather was unfaithful. Most people would perhaps assume that his behavior would lead to constant arguments or tension within the household. Conversely, that was never the case. My grandmother always treated him with such respect. This only deepened my confusion because her response was never indicative of a woman scorned or bitter surrounding her husband's dishonor toward their marriage vows.

I viewed everything through the lens of my emotions which distorted the true picture of what was happening around me.

Despite the pain she must have felt, my grandmother never raised her voice nor reacted to my grandfather's behavior in a negative or derogatory manner. She simply stayed on her knees in prayer, even as she aged and could no longer physically kneel. She continued unwavering in her devotion to the Lord. I now realize she was a prayer warrior, a pillar of strength in the face of adversity. Her conduct during those times was remarkable, although I didn't appreciate it then. I honestly mistook her grace for weakness, thinking she was a pushover. But she would often say, "Two wrongs will never make a right." As I matured in life, I started to realize her heart posture reflected deep wisdom.

The differences between my father's and grandmother's houses were not about the unfortunate negative atmosphere. The real difference was the presence of God, all due to my precious grandmother's deep love and devotion to Him. Amazingly, she fully committed her life to the Lord despite her situation. For so long, I believed my struggle was tied to not living with my biological family. This was compounded by the fact that no one ever truly explained the reasons why. This was the reality I knew, but it wasn't the complete truth. The real truth was something I had to discover on my own as I grew in my personal relationship with the Lord.

As I matured, I began to see the reasons for my placement with my grandparents were part of a divine plan. The Lord used this situation to bring me into a greater understanding of His will and purpose for my life. This realization didn't come overnight — it was a journey filled with spiritual turmoil and emotional upheaval. I didn't fully grasp how the actions of the adults in my life, whom I called family, impacted my spiritual well-being. My one constant element was the relationship my grandmother had with the Lord. It was this relationship which created my opening to be drawn to Him as well.

During my formative years, the sense of being an outsider in my own family weighed heavily on me. I often felt like a puzzle piece that didn't quite fit. I experienced this unsettling feeling not only in my father's chaotic household, but also in my grandparents' home. The latter was felt despite the peaceful facade that most would believe was the truth. The silence in my grandmother's home was sometimes more unsettling than the noise in my father's. It was a silence filled with unspoken pain, unasked questions, and even unresolved conflicts. Yet, it was also a silence where I first heard the whisper of God's voice calling me to something greater.

I struggled with feelings of abandonment and rejection, wondering why I had been chosen to live away from my parents. This sense of rejection was compounded by the lack of transparency about my situation. As a child, I longed for clarity, for someone to sit down and explain to me why things were the way they were. But those answers never came, at least not in the way I expected. Instead, I had to learn to live with the ambiguity and subsequently make peace with the silence.

It wasn't until I matured in the things of God for myself that I began to understand my grandmother's home was not just a place of refuge... it was a place of unspoken pain. Regardless, I can attest it was there where my faith was forged. Her unwavering faith in God, even in the face of my grandfather's infidelity, became a beacon of light. She never preached or forced her beliefs on me nor my grandfather. Her life was a testament to the power of prayer and the strength that comes from a deep, abiding faith in God. Her actions truly spoke louder than words.

As I grew older and began to explore my own personal relationship with the Father, I realized my grandmother's quiet strength was not weakness. It was a profound expression of her trust in God's plan. She understood something which took me years to comprehend. She demonstrated *what* she believed. She knew that sometimes our greatest battles must be fought on our knees in prayer... not with raised voices or harsh words. Her example taught me the importance of grace under pressure. She also demonstrated integrity and dignity, even when life was not fair.

My journey toward understanding my identity and purpose was not a straightforward path. It was filled with detours, doubts, and moments of despair. Yet, it was also a journey of discovery, where I slowly began to see the hand of God at work in my life. I started to recognize the struggles I had faced were not just random occurrences, but part of a larger tapestry that God was weaving together for my good.

One of the most significant lessons I learned was the importance of forgiveness. I had harbored so much anger and resentment toward my parents for the perceived abandonment. I also felt deep, not-so-positive emotions toward my grandfather for his betrayal of my grandmother. Holding onto that anger was like drinking poison and expecting the other person to die. It was only through the grace of God that I was able to let go of that bitterness and embrace forgiveness.

Forgiveness did not come easily, nor did it happen overnight. It was a process which required me to confront my pain, sit with it, and allow God to heal those wounds. I had to learn to forgive not just my parents and grandfather, but also myself for the anger and resentment I had carried for so long. This act of forgiveness was not about condoning their actions. It was more about freeing myself from the chains of bitterness that had me bound.

In the process of forgiving, I also had to learn to trust God's plan for my life. This was perhaps the hardest lesson of all because it required me to surrender my desire for control and to accept that I might never fully understand why things happened the way they did. Trusting God meant believing He had a purpose for my pain and could bring beauty out of the ashes of my brokenness.

As I continued to grow in my faith, I began to see my testimony was not just about me. It was part of a larger narrative God was writing, a story of redemption and grace. My experiences, both good and bad, had shaped me into the person I was becoming. They'd given me a unique perspective. It was a viewpoint that allowed me to empathize and easily extend grace to others who were going through similar struggles.

My relationship with the Lord became the foundation upon which I built my life. It was not an easy road, but it was one filled with lessons I would carry with me for the rest of my life. The most important of these was the realization that my identity was not defined by my circumstances, nor was it exemplified by the actions of others. It was defined by who I was in Christ: I am a child of God.

The journey I had embarked on was one of transformation. It was a journey from brokenness to wholeness, from despair to hope, from anger to forgiveness. It was a journey that took me from being a victim of my circumstances to being a victor in Christ. It was a journey I knew would continue for the rest of my life, growing in my relationship with God.

As I look back on my life, I can see the fingerprints of God all over my story. I can see how He took the pain and confusion of my childhood and used it to shape me into the person I am today. I can see how He brought people like my grandmother into my life, to guide me and to show me what it means to live a life of faith. I can acknowledge He has been with me every step of the way, even when I didn't realize it.

Chapter 12

The Challenge

What is the purpose behind everything I've shared so far? That's a good question. Many people believe leaders always have their lives together, and this enables them to lead others through their thought process. This couldn't be further from the truth. Every true leader faces challenges. The Father uses these challenges to help prepare them for leadership. I wanted to make this real by sharing my personal walk with the Lord. I am hopeful this will encourage and challenge you to reflect on your own stories. The reality is we all have significant moments in our lives which deeply impact us. But truthfully, our testimonies are not always silver-lined; some come from beaten and broken places.

My ultimate goal is to simply expose my vulnerabilities for your benefit as you explore your own story. Over the years, I've learned an effective leader steps out front and invites others to follow. Their heart should always be humbly postured, allowing followers to learn and grow from their mistakes and vulnerabilities. This creates a space where everyone can grow together. So, my account is really an invitation for you to push past fear, anger, grief, doubt, or anything else that may be blocking you from experiencing freedom. I had many challenges as a child, and most of these challenges can be traced back to family dynamics. The adults in my family could have easily explained the reasons for my living situation. Unfortunately, no one took the lead. The good news is the "not-so-positive" experiences allowed a transformation in my heart so I can now see life clearly through the lens of the Father.

It's been so enlightening to gain this clarity. I never realized how much my story had influenced the optics of my heart. I learned I'd been focusing on environment and culture and not the Truth of God's Word. This growth process has allowed me to discover my own strengths as a leader and as an effective communicator. I am keenly aware of the importance communications plays in our lives. It's become my passion to help others to do the same.

The enemy often preys on our feelings, trying to control our minds with facts that may seem true but aren't *the* Truth. You probably have your own version of *truth*. We all do. For example, *"If I'd been good enough, things would have turned out differently."* This is typical. These thoughts, while powerful, are not reality and are fueled by emotions. They shape our lives in ways which can hold us back from living a victorious life in Christ as the Father intended. It's crucial to recognize and replace these false narratives with the truth that sets you free. But this isn't just about inner battles; it's also about the words we speak (or fail to speak) into the lives of others, especially our children.

The things we say to our children carry weight, but the things we *don't* say can carry even more. The enemy exploits our silence during those times we avoid saying things like, *"I love you,"* or *"It's not your fault… things will work out."* A parent's words are vital to the development of a child's heart, mind, and confidence.

We can't keep doing things the same way and expect different results — that's the definition of insanity. It's essential to recognize that real change begins with acknowledging the issues in our lives and uncovering their root causes. This is the only way to truly influence the lives of others and create lasting impact. Based on many testimonies from those I've pastored or coached, my leadership style and communication skills are the main reasons I've been influential in their lives. Yet admittedly, that would never have been the case had I not first surrendered to the process of discovering the root causes of my own issues.

The feelings and pain we experience often point to something deeper. Just as the prayers of a loved one can provide protection and strength, it's crucial to understand the power of prayer and faith while seeking Truth. Remember, as Romans 8:28 assures us, our heavenly Father is always working everything together for our good. His desire is to teach, strengthen, and empower us to grow in His Truth, which is found in His Word.

During an altar ministry encounter about seven years ago, I really began to experience the Father's heart deeply. It was a pivotal moment in my life and ministry. It was the encounter that allowed me to really receive the Father's unconditional love toward me as His son. This became the catalyst for the healing of my heart. It's so profoundly interesting that at the time, I didn't even realize my heart needed healing. I believe this is the case with most if not all of us. Until we recognize the adversary's plots to skew the optics (viewpoint) of our hearts, we will be unable to see the brokenness or the need to receive healing. (Ephesians 1:18a, *"the eyes of your understanding being enlightened."*

In my case, I had always thought that as a leader, my initial response should be: *"I'm good; I'm trusting*

God by faith." It was not until my encounter that I recognized typically when a believer in Christ makes statements like these, it reveals wounds; it indicates unresolved issues. Yet the great news is our Father is patiently waiting for us to receive all He created us to be and acquire.

However, there's one certainty: the enemy will *never* tell you the truth. He doesn't want you to become aware of the emotional impact of an absent parent or a parent who doesn't step up to lead their family forward in truth. My personal family drama distorted my view of myself, my family, and the Father. When this happens, everything else in our lives becomes distorted as well. Honestly, this likely occurs in nearly every household on some level.

So, the challenge becomes whether we are willing to allow the Holy Spirit to expose those areas of our hearts. If the answer is "Yes," then we are not only communicating to the Father that we're surrendering our will to His, but we're accepting the responsibility to break the cycles of brokenness within our families. Once we admit the need and embrace God's desire to heal the deep places of our hearts, things begin to become clearer. The Holy Spirit will start to expose areas causing continued emotional pain. As He leads us into His Truth, we'll then begin to ask ourselves questions like, *"Have I forgiven those who have hurt me in my family or in other broken relationships from my past?"* Or perhaps, *"Am I continuing to blame others for my poor decisions and choices?"*

These are just a few examples of questions that can help expose areas in need of healing. During this process, it may be necessary to ask others for forgiveness as awareness of any lingering unforgiveness grows. However, please remember this should never involve conversations with people who have violent tendencies. Your safety is paramount — never put yourself in harm's way.

Reflecting on my experiences, I realized the absence of leadership within my family wasn't just a personal struggle; it was an issue which affects many households worldwide. God calls certain ones to be leaders in the Church. But leaders are only human and will fall short and even fail at times. This typically causes confusion, elevates doubt, and can instill an unstable environment rippling through every aspect of life. This has given me a unique perspective on what true leadership should look like in the context of family.

Good leadership in a family begins with taking ownership and responsibility. This should not only include a parent's or significant adult guardian's day-to-day interactions, it should also include nurturing the growth and ensuring the wellbeing of every family member. Leadership and family accountability at this level involves setting a standard of behavior, godly values, and virtuous principles rooted in love, respect, and understanding. A true leader in the family doesn't shy away from hard conversations or difficult decisions. Instead, they confront challenges head-on, always considering the impact on those they are guiding. They understand leadership is less about authority and more about service — serving their family with patience, kindness, and wisdom.

To lead effectively, a family leader must model integrity and consistency. Through their actions, they should demonstrate what it means to live a life guided by biblical principles and aligned with the Father's original design and purpose. This means demonstrating humility, being willing to admit mistakes, seek forgiveness, and make amends when necessary. It also means nurturing an environment where every family member feels safe to express themselves, so communication can flow openly and freely. In other words, they create an environment where the agape love of Christ is the foundation of every interaction. When a parent or guardian leads with empathy and humility, they create a space where trust can flourish, children feel valued, and growth becomes a shared, life-giving journey.

Moreover, a good family leader recognizes the spiritual dimension of their role. It becomes an essential and often pivotal place for transformational leadership in the family. It also creates a trajectory for generational blessings and a wholesome family legacy. Once you understand your actions and decisions will holistically shape a child's physical, emotional, and spiritual well-being, then leading the family effectively through prayer and faith will become a way of life! You will become your family's role model in seeking God's guidance, relying on His wisdom, and demonstrating a life surrendered to Christ.

Life is so precious, so sharing one's faith journey encourages the family to pursue their own relationship with God. This spiritual leadership model based on biblical principles provides a solid foundation the family can stand on, even in the face of life's inevitable storms. Moving forward, you will begin to see the qualities of good family leadership is not just an idealistic aspiration, but is a practical, everyday lifestyle. A leader in the family should embody both strength and gentleness, firmness and flexibility. They should be able to stand firm in their convictions while being willing to listen, learn, and adapt. Good leadership is not about being perfect; it's about being present, available, and willing to grow alongside those you are guiding. If it is rooted in the agape love of our Father, you will even extend love, grace, and godly-based values to your relationships outside the family.

In my own journey, it was indeed a phenomenal breakthrough experience once I embraced this principle that true family leadership is essential to have a successful life. It breaks off limitations, eliminates victimhood, and transforms mindsets so we can embrace vulnerability as a strength, not a weakness.

I encourage you to join me in being open and vulnerable moving forward. It's not just ok to share your own struggles, mistakes, and lessons learned. It's highly important to *embrace* it as part of great leadership in your family, community, and beyond. Let's step up and fill the gaps others have left unchallenged. Prayerfully seek the Father as His beloved son or daughter by being willing to break cycles of pain, dysfunction, and neglect which may have persisted for generations in your families. It's so empowering! Without realizing it, you'll begin a new legacy of love, faith, and resilience where every family member is empowered to lead in their own way. Everyone becomes "one in His Spirit," and the family unit becomes the manifestation of Jesus' prayer in John 17:21, "*...that they all may be one, as You, Father, are in Me, and I in You; that they also may be one in Us, that the world may believe that You sent Me.*"

Our steps will not only be ordered by the Father, but also will be guided by a deep sense of purpose and a commitment to something greater than ourselves. In essence, good leadership in a family isn't about exercising control or demanding obedience. It's about fostering a culture of mutual respect, shared values, and collective growth. It's about recognizing each family member has a role to play, and the true strength of a family lies in its unity and its diversity.

Now that this book is near conclusion, please take time to reflect... Pray... Seek the Lord for more insight and wisdom on how to move forward with these principles in mind. For me, I needed to really reflect on my grandparents' example of family leadership (or lack thereof). I learned not to focus on the negative experiences, but to instead dive into biblical wisdom and revelation for application of the life lessons learned. I am reminded every family has the potential to be a place of healing, growth, and love. It all begins with the decision to lead with intention, guided by a humble, open, and faith-filled heart.

Thank you for reading this book
"The Lens of The Father."
If you were blessed by the book or his ministry and would like to follow Dennis G. Lindsay on social media or invite him to speak at your upcoming event, here's how you can contact Dennis.

thelensofthefather.com

or email

dgl@thelensofthefather.com

www.ingramcontent.com/pod-product-compliance
Lightning Source LLC
Chambersburg PA
CBHW070204100426
42743CB00013B/3048